BROKEN. MESSY. LOVED.

BROKEN.
MESSY.
LOVED.

Heather Bost

Names have been changed to protect the identities of the persons involved.

Paperback ISBN: 978-1-64999-317-5

Ebook ISBN: 9781649450425

TABLE OF CONTENTS

DEDICATION

To my ma and pops.
My forever thumb buddy and shoulder to lean on.
Mom, your love is fierce. Dad, your strength is
admirable.

To my five siblings.
You are strong, brave, and beautiful.
So blessed for your support in all my endeavors, even
the crazy ones.

Nicholas, Alexander, Joey, Gianna, and Riley
Your light and growth are inspiring.

INTRODUCTION

The vase crashed to the floor in the most ungraceful way, glass scattering in every direction. The sound was loud and obtrusive, breaking the silence. What was once a beautifully handcrafted piece of art shattered, leaving behind a mess. Pieces lay around recklessly, ready to cut anyone that entered the kitchen.

Would someone come to sweep it up or attempt to put it back together? Or would it sit there on the kitchen floor, now useless and forgotten? It would be impossible to piece it back together. Could it ever be the shape that its creator once made it?

"Heather!" The snapping of my mother's fingers brought me out of my trance, where the broken flower vase was now sprayed across the tile. Before I dumped the remains into the trash, I paused, staring into the reflective shards.

I was using the vase as a drinking cup—strange, I know. It broke because I was clumsy. It also broke because I was not using it for its intended purpose. Too many times in my life did I feel comparable to this vase, finding myself in other people's hands, being used for purposes never meant. Too many times I was left broken on the floor, finding myself alone in places I should have never been in the first place. Too often I found myself causing a mess and either getting thrown away or never quite put back together the same, cutting people that came close because I myself was broken.

The more fixing I tried to do, the more scarred and damaged I became, always seeking "healing" from the next quick fix until there was no more putting me back together and broken I stayed. It was not until I messed around and heard about Jesus that my life radically changed.

Although I grew up in a lovely house with amazing parents and siblings, I did not grow up in a house of faith. I was uncertain of the church, the Bible, and only knew how to recite a prayer over my food. Shame, guilt, and unworthiness took place in my heart. When I would recall all the things I had done or all the crappy things that had been done to me, it did not make sense. How could God be "for" me? How could He love me? How could He have a plan for me in this state? I was broken, messy, and mad at the world. My vision of myself was distorted, as if I were looking into the shattered glass that was once a functional vase.

If you look into the mirror, what do you see? Do you see bits and pieces of your damaged past? Do you see the scars and tears left behind from many different seasons of life? Do shame and guilt weigh heavy on your shoulders? Do you stare at the person in the mirror and disqualify yourself from the love of God? Is your biggest Goliath the one staring back at you?

Then let us begin the journey. In the pages to come, I want to simply share my transparent testimony with you: moments in time that God used and restored my mess and brokenness. I want to show you a sneak peek of tools I used to defeat my Goliaths, how God took me in the state I was in and transformed my life, and how He continues to do so each day.

As you read these pages, I pray that God reveals Himself to you in a new, beautiful way. I also pray that God shows you how He sees you, stripping away the labels placed on you and helping you change one day at a time the distorted view you might see in the mirror. By the end of this book, I pray you can live from a place of overflow rather than a place of deficit and you can see who God has made you to be despite all your mistakes. You are His masterpiece. He had a plan for you written before you were even born. The goal of these pages is for you to choose to love who God has handmade you to be.

Before you pick this book up each day, ask God to open your heart to Him. Ask Him to speak to you and show you the parts that need healing. Be transparent with Him, and let the transformation begin.

CHAPTER 1

LABELED "DO NOT OPEN"

Have you ever felt like you wanted to melt into the floor? Wished that in a millisecond you could vanish into thin air, escaping reality in front of you? Have you ever thought about hitting the imaginary switch on your chest, shutting off your brain and even more so your breaking heart?

I want to know who in the world came up with the saying "follow your heart" because I would most definitely want to have a discussion with them. It is pretty clear in Scripture to not go chasing after your heart. "The heart is deceitful above all things, and desperately sick; who can understand it?" (Jer. 17:9).

Ignoring my brain, I followed my heart all right, giving it to the "bad boy" Steven. He was the talk of the school. He was just getting back from a long suspension for punching the principal and just so happened to sit next to me in the cafeteria. We became friends throughout middle school and stayed that way for a while. Although I was most definitely crushing on him, he did not have the best track record. But he could change, right? Students could be spreading rumors; he wasn't that bad, right? I ignored his reputation and pursued to have a relationship with him.

Finally, one day he called my house phone and asked me if I wanted to be his girlfriend! I was so happy I let out a squeal when I clicked off the phone. We could live happily ever after, be the next Disney remake.

Wrong.

We could not do that due to the fact he arrived at the skating rink a week later with my best friend, having the nerve to even hold her hand around the rink, telling me he liked her and was dumping me.

That was the first time my heart actually felt like it hurt. Steven, how could you? I was so embarrassed and felt more insecure than ever. *So dramatic*, you might be thinking. But you tell that to a middle-school girl who believed in fairy tales and true love, who put her heart in her hand and gave it away to the boy that made her feel special, hoping that one day he might want it.

I didn't understand the love I was trying to find would never be found in the form of a man, much less a boy. The pattern continued, and the heart tears kept ripping away bit by bit.

From a young age, I was very passionate. I loved to love. I was very intense, like the psalmist David in the Bible. I love poetry and expressing myself, from one minute of jumping for joy on the mountaintop to the next minute doubling over in pain in the valley. I threw everything I had into relationships, giving 100 percent in all the things I did.

From sleeping beauties to princes, kissing toads to sweeping chimneys, you name it, I watched it. Not sure why I wanted to be a princess that bad, but if I could sleep in my Cinderella costume, all was right in the world. Each one of these tales I admired so much was a story of love. Deep, mountain-moving, dragon-slaying love. It was as if all my adolescence I was searching for the need to be loved unconditionally. I thought the attention of the relationships I was in was the love I longed for, and that was why I suffered so deeply. Little did I know that I already had it—God already loved me.

Ephesians 1:4 (NLT) says, "Even before he made the world, God loved us and chose us in Christ to be holy and without fault in his eyes." This is what I was searching for: my creator's love that was already poured over me. His love is an unconditional, never-failing, mountain-moving, monster-slaying type of love. A love that looks at you without fault. A love that lasts. But I was building my foundations on fairy tales and the very misleading ways of the world. It was as if I had a massive void in my heart and I was determined to fill it—only I was placing it in all the wrong places, not in God.

Let me set the record straight here and now: do not "follow your heart." Scripture says our hearts are deceitful and wicked. I have seen that to be true—my heart was so deceitful, and many times it was wicked. Proverbs 4:23 says, "Above all else, guard your heart, for everything you do flows from it." I wasn't guarding my heart at all. In fact, I was giving it away willingly to those that definitely did not need to have it. I left my heart unguarded and vulnerable. I went from boy to boy, hoping that one might stick.

As I continued down the path of self-sabotage, my unguarded heart let many things in. And like the Scripture says, what came in began to flow out. Depression began to form. It took the stage in my mind. Insecurity gripped me, and I started listening to all the lies whispering inside. I began to self-isolate myself. I was so afraid to be rejected by other kids that I would take my lunch into the school bathroom and eat in the stall. Or sometimes I would skip school altogether to avoid the fact I felt as if no one understood me. There was nothing more daunting to me than being alone in a crowd full of people and noise.

Sometimes I look in the mirror today and I can see that little girl eating in the bathroom stall. That little girl who was afraid of the world. Who would cry and cry, not even knowing why she was so sad, feeling weak and ashamed. Who felt lost, alone, and longed to feel whole. Who struggled to find her worth in the world around her, not understanding she was not going to find it there. I might be twenty-seven years old now and have learned a great deal since then, but that little girl is still in me. She is still a part of me.

The first thing I want to tell you is: do not hide parts of yourself. Do not lock away the parts of yourself others might look at you differently for if only they knew. The parts that you think are unlovable, that seem to disqualify you. The parts you keep pushing back like they aren't there: the abuse, the depression, the heartbreak, the failure, the loss. The parts the world says "time will heal."

Friend, time does not heal all. There are some things that only Jesus can heal, things that no medicine, no remedy, nothing of this world can fix. Pushing these things away can make an un-dealt-with pain turn into a silent, raging monster that starts off as one incident or one emotion or one affliction, then slowly grows from pain to anger to depression or bitterness.

My unmanaged emotions were building up inside of me like a soda with the cap on that kept getting shaken, ready to explode when finally opened.

It might have been years ago that I felt this way, alone, lost, and insecure, but that little girl still stared back at me in the mirror from time to time. She never stayed in middle school, she came right to high school, and she tried to follow me in the beginning of college. Now, six years later at twenty-seven, I would still have to push her away. "That's not me anymore," I would repeat again and again. I felt ashamed that I even remembered those days. It made me feel weak that sometimes, when I thought about it, it still made me sad and confused.

I gave my life to Christ at an Easter service in 2011. God did not instantly cure me of everything that I was struggling with, and that little me liked to pop in. Like times I would go to teach a sermon at a life group, or when I would lead in prayer on Sundays; times when I would do devotionals to kick off the hospitality team, or when I would write. She loved to pop up during moments that I needed confidence, moments that I was going against all that insecurity.

One day as I was preparing for my first teaching in front of a good-sized youth group of middle- and high-school kids, she appeared. I was backstage the day before praying for wisdom and confidence when I looked up in the mirror. I saw this fragile little girl who stumbled on her words and hid in the background. I knew right then and there it was time to stop pushing my insecurity away. It was part of my past no matter how far I had come. I realized I never even gave that part of me over to God, just ignored it like it wasn't there.

The problem was I was ashamed of feeling that way, so I did not allow God to help me in it. I thought I could just handle it on my own. I was a grown-up now! I loved the Lord, and He loved me! But the shame and guilt were having their way. I knew if God was going to use all of me, I needed to confront these parts of myself and surrender them over. If I wanted this insecure little girl to stop jumping in, if I wanted to stop giving my past the power to keep me from my future, I had to give it to Jesus. 1 Peter 5:7 (NLT) says, "Give all your worries and cares to God, for he cares about you." Psalm 55:22 says, "Cast your burden upon the LORD and He will sustain you; He will never allow the righteous to be shaken." I had to bring this to Him. I knew that in order to teach little girls that might be feeling this exact way, I had to confront the old me. In order to be affective at sharing my testimony and speaking to those hurting around me, I had to surrender it.

I know I am not the only one the past tries to haunt, that I am not alone when old pains try to dictate my future. If this is you and that moment, that pain, that insecurity, that thing you wish you could forget when it comes to mind, allow it. Instead of pushing it away again, confront it, allow Jesus into it, because that pain is still a part of you whether you want to admit it or not.

There is no erasing the past. It is part of what makes you who you are. You get to decide what part it plays. Is it a part that Jesus uses, or one that haunts you? When I gave Jesus permission into that part of my past and stopped trying to ignore it, then the healing process began.

As I was spending time in prayer and in the word, I came upon Psalm 139. I had this beautiful thought of what Jesus would say to that little me. He would meet me there right in that bathroom stall, bend down, cradle my little chin in His hands, and look me right in the eyes. I can see Him gently wiping the tears away. I imagine He would say something like Psalm 139 over me in a sincere, compassionate, fatherly tone. "My little girl. You are beautifully made. I know that you might feel alone, but I was here all along. You never leave my sight. I am here in the stall, in class, even at home. I know when you come in here and when you leave. I am with you in secret places. I know every hair on your head and collect all those tears you cry into your pillow. The plan I have for your life is far beyond those fairy tales, you watch. Even in this darkness, the light will shine through. Just hang in there, and keep fighting those lies in your head. I am here. What I have put down on the inside of you is worth more than you know. I wrote down your days, and not even this one will be wasted. Even this time that seems unbearable will be a faint memory in years to come. Just you wait. You, my little one, are special, you will see."

When I see that girl in the mirror, I can now smile and remember Jesus was there all along. I can smile because He is faithful every step of the way, even when I do not see Him.

What part of you on the inside needs to hear that? What part of you needs to know that He was there all along? What part do you keep pushing down but God wants to speak to? He wants you to know that He loves that part of you, too, the insecure one, the depressed one, the part you put a mask over, the one that still stings when you think about it. There is healing available for that part too. Stop hiding it, and let Him into it. He can't fix what you fake. God can't bless who you pretend to be, and acknowledging pain does not make you weak. It allows Jesus to make you stronger. For when we are weak, He is strong (2 Cor. 12:9).

It takes courage to dig out those parts in your heart. It takes strength to admit you need to revisit and heal. God wants into that place. Will you allow Him? Do not allow the past to label your present. I know the emotions are tucked way back in there, put in that box labeled "do not open." Let Him open the box and remove them.

God cannot bless who you pretend to be.

Psalm 139 helps me find the courage to let Him in. These scriptures remind me how much He cares for me every step of the way. Even if I did not see Him or feel Him, He was always working on my behalf. His love endures even during my most painful moments.

Take some time before we move forward and meditate on these scriptures. Pray it over yourself. Read it out loud. I dare you to pray a dangerous prayer asking Him into the deepest, darkest parts of you and giving Him the authority over all areas of your heart. You might not "feel" anything at first, but I am confident transformation will occur with this consistent confession.

PRAYER:

Heavenly Father, here I am. I come to you in truth and surrender. I need you desperately. I know you see into my heart and into my thoughts. You know the things that I would not utter to anyone, and you love me just the same. You love me past the mistakes I have made and for the ones I will make in the future. I am so thankful for your love because you say that nothing can separate you from me. When everything else seems to be failing, you will never fail me.

Search my heart, Lord, and show me anything I need your healing power in. I am tired and worn out from trying to do this on my own. You say to draw near to you and that you will draw near to me. I do not have it figured out, but you do. Take the burdens, Lord, I cast them at your feet. Thank you for saying that your yoke is light. Thank you for being an ever-present help in times of trouble. I take the step and open up every area of my life to you, even the messy ones. Have your way, Lord. In Jesus's name, amen.

You have searched me, Lord, and you know me. You know when I sit and when I rise; you perceive my thoughts from afar. You discern my going out and my lying down; you are familiar with all my ways.

Before a word is on my tongue, you, Lord, know it completely. You hem me in behind and before, and you lay your hand upon me. Such knowledge is too wonderful for me, too lofty for me to attain.

Where can I go from your Spirit? Where can I flee from your presence? If I go up to the heavens, you are there; if I make my bed in the depths, you are there. If I rise on the wings of the dawn, if I settle on the far side of the sea, even there your hand will guide me, your right hand will hold me fast.

If I say, "Surely the darkness will hide me and the light become night around me," even the darkness will not be dark to you; the night will shine like the day, for darkness is as light to you.

For you created my inmost being; you knit me together in my mother's womb. I praise you because I am fearfully and wonderfully made; your works are wonderful. I know that full well.

My frame was not hidden from you when I was made in the secret place, when I was woven together in the depths of the earth. Your eyes saw my unformed body; all the days ordained for me were written in your book before one of them came to be.

How precious to me are your thoughts, God! How vast is the sum of them! Were I to count them, they would outnumber the grains of sand—when I awake, I am still with you.

—Psalm 139:1–18

CHAPTER 2

THE C-WORD

Allow me to drop you smack-dab into 2009. My eyes were drifting here and there, following a fly racing around the waiting room. There I was sitting in the hospital picturing myself as a fly, imagining myself soaring carelessly around the waiting room, buzzing from magazine to coffee cup to half-eaten orange and trying to get my tiny insect legs on anything.

I wonder what flies are searching for. They never seem to be satisfied with what they land on. Are they ever full? How much can that little guy eat? Does he even get afraid when people swat at him, threatening his very life? Does he have a family, and does he ever miss them?

A fly on the wall. Yes, that was what I wanted to be right now. My mind flooded with silly thoughts of that little fly. Did you know that insects can last several days without a head? Maybe I was turning into a fly after all. My head did not feel attached to my shoulders these past few days. I had to reach up to make sure it was still there. Who knows, when the earthquake hit my house, it might have swallowed up my head.

There was an earthquake that occurred right there in my living room, sending tremors into the depths of every nerve cell in my body, leaving nothing unshaken. When the "family meeting" was called, I immediately started going down the list of what I did wrong that week and how on earth they caught me. One of my sisters must have snitched me out, or maybe the school called, crap.

Except this was no ordinary meeting of skipping school or sneaking out. Instead it was a meeting where they dropped the C-word. Cancer was the earthquake that hit on that ordinary day, turning me into a headless fly in the hospital family room.

"We can estimate about four months left with the severity of the spreading. We might be able to get him more time with surgery, but there is no guarantee…"

My attention flipped from the frantic fly to the dude wearing a coat. I wanted to fight him. Who did he think he was, and how could he say that? Where were his credentials? Where did he even go to school? Did he know who he was talking about? It wasn't just some patient—it was my dad!

Time stood still. The moment his gut-punching words of "four months" came out, I wanted to make him take them all back, wanted to laugh and say this was all a misunderstanding, he must have gotten the wrong chart.

How did this happen? My dad is my best friend. My wrestling partner who was the current standing steamroller champion of the Bost house. My mother's rock. He was fun, creative, and full of childlike energy. How could this be?

Four months? I didn't even know he was sick to begin with. I was only sixteen—I needed him. There were so many things we still had to do. Boys that he would have to protect me from. An aisle he had to walk me down one day. He had to come to the rescue when my siblings were out to get me. There were so many daddy-daughter days to come.

Life took an abrupt turn in 2009 when Pops, my hero, was diagnosed with stage-three esophageal cancer. It was aggressive cancer, to say the least.

The hospital became an all-too-familiar place. At least I could hide there in the maze of hallways and tucked-away rooms. In the beginning, our home became the place to avoid. My mother was trying to keep it all together. How she managed was beyond me. I think we all aged years in those few months. We happened to find a doctor that was willing to operate and do a surgery that had never been done before. I knew if anyone could survive it that it would be my pops. And that he did.

What they don't tell you is that the cancer is not the hard part. It is the road to recovery that will be etched in my memories forever. It is the chemotherapy after that will leave you questioning, "Is this even treatment? Is he even better? Why is there so much pain?"

Seeing him in the ICU after the surgery took me to the floor. When I finally got to go in, the wind escaped my body as if I were a balloon losing its helium. I quickly excused myself, found the nearest exit, and let the tears rain onto the floor. When I finally found use of my legs, I went back in and put on my big-girl face. I could barely see him, there was so much equipment attached to him. He looked like an alien. There were more tubes and machines than there was man. He was frail and zombieish, like at any moment he would get off the bed and chase us, lusting for life. I was afraid that when he woke up everything would be changed as we knew it. I was afraid that the man who went in that surgery room was never coming back out.

They said it was good for us to talk around him, for him to hear our voices, but every time I tried, nothing could come out except a scratchy sound and tears. I wanted to be strong—strong for my mom, strong for my sisters and brother, strong for him. But he was always the one that was strong! I choked back every emotion, casting it all away, locking it on that shelf in my mind that was labeled "avoid at all costs."

Recovery was a whole other animal. I felt selfish at this stage because I could not bear it. I would rather be home cleaning for my mom or making dinner for the family, anything to avoid the hospital visits. Every time I saw my dad in pain, it was like nails to a chalkboard, but nothing could make the scraping noise stop. My dad is the toughest man I know; this was a whole new sight for me. To see him cry or yell in pain felt as if it were causing me physical pain.

Be strong, be strong. If he can do this, you can do this. The words continued echoing in my head. I would have done anything to take it away from him. The common question alone at night was *why*? Why was this happening?

After he did wake up, you think I would have been jumping for joy. But in reality, I was more afraid than ever. He could not talk for a while and was not allowed to eat or drink. He was not allowed to have *any* liquids under strict orders from the doctor. He was on a lot of drugs and was going kind of crazy. Okay, a lot of crazy. He would beg me for things he could not have and try to persuade me the doctors were trying to kill him in the night. He would tell me that I must not love him or else I would help him. He was convinced that I hated him because I would not give him ice chips that I knew he could not have.

I knew that he did not mean the things he would say, but it did not take away their stabs. It did not take away the fact I wanted to make everything better, put him in the car and drive far, far away, or grab a cape, put it around my neck, swoop in, and save the day. I wanted my dad back, the one whom all the doctors wheeled behind those swinging doors.

He was in recovery for quite some time, but the doctor said he was doing great. My mind said otherwise. I wanted the days back before that ugly sickness got to our family. The days before it stole things from us we would not get back.

Once we got him home, it was not any easier. He had a tube in his stomach where he would get nutrients from until he healed more. I knew he wanted to give up at that point, getting fed through a tube and all the complications that came with it. Who could blame him? Every day seemed to be a fight. Infections kept causing him a lot of pain. One evening I walked into my mother's room to find him ripping the tube out of his stomach, begging for us to just take it out, saying he would rather be dead than go through the pain every day. The rest of his recovery became a blur.

I wish I could tell you that this was where I found God, but that would not be the truth. In honesty, I did not drop to my knees and pray. I did not open a Bible. I did not know much about God then, much less that He was in control even in that storm. I did not see evidence of His presence as the hope for "normal" to return back to our family drifted away. I was angry.

When I was in the middle of this season, I did not see God anywhere. I saw pain and loss, trauma and avoidance. I felt that my dad was taken from me in a sense. I was hurt and confused by the events of life. At sixteen, I found myself asking, "What kind of God would allow this?"

I took all the emotions, and I locked them away; no one knew what a toll this season took on me. I am sure each person in my family could connect in that way, but we did not talk about it, just hid it on that shelf in the deep cabinet that was getting pretty crowded. Maybe time could just wash it away.

But time did not wash it away. Instead it grew into a giant monster in the room, one that no one would confront, one who would surface later in a new, terrifying way.

Now, eleven years later, as I look back, I can see God was all over. If it weren't for Him, a different outcome would have most certainly taken place. He was upholding us with His victorious right hand. God was getting us out of bed, keeping us fed, strengthening us to be there watching the ugly chemo process, helping us to be there to support my mother and father in every way we could. He was there as the doctors removed cancer from my dad's damaged body, turning man's words of four months to ten years strong. God was there all along, even if I did not see Him.

Life is full of shattering moments. God is there for every single one of them. We might not feel or see it, but He is there.

One of the many things I love about Jesus is that He is not just some cheerleader standing on the sidelines yelling at you, "Come on! Keep running! You got this!" He is not standing there looking at you, holding a sign as the massive defensive line knocks the wind out of you. He is on the field with you, running the play with you, getting down in the mess with you. He is Immanuel, God with us. In these heartbreaking moments, that is the truth you must cling to. He is right alongside you holding you up. He is behind you pushing you forward. He is in front of you clearing the path.

Psalm 46:1–3 (ESV) says, "God is our refuge and strength, a very present help in trouble. Therefore we will not fear though the earth gives way, though the mountains be moved into the heart of the sea, though its waters roar and foam, though the mountains tremble at its swelling." There might be obstacles in front of you, roaring and foaming, looking as though any moment now they are going to consume you. There might be things happening that look as if God is nowhere to be found. But the truth is He is a very present help in trouble. He is close to the brokenhearted and those crushed in spirit. Those are promises made to you. And no season, no heartache, no sickness, no death can take away the truth of God's word.

These moments that try to devastate you, that seem to paralyze you from moving forward, are moments of shaping. Crushing moments are not supposed to be the end of us. Despite what it seems, they are shaping us, directing us, building us, crushing to create, crushing to make space for new.

When we experience this, we often want to seek answers. That was what I wanted: answers. Why was this happening? What did he do to deserve this? If I could gain understanding, then maybe I could gain control. I was looking for answers around me that I would never find. Instead of finding refuge in God, I spiraled further down into depression.

My family's run-in with cancer was not meant to defeat us, and it did not despite how hard it tried. The crushing was positioning us. We were not being punished. We were not being forgotten. We were being positioned, getting pruned and prepared for the next season of life.

If you are in the middle of a crushing moment, then I pray you can look and find God in it. That you can look to the Scripture and find comfort knowing He is in the middle with you. You are not alone—you are surrounded by Him. If I had known that at the time, then maybe I could have avoided what was to come next in my life, but maybe not.

There is no earth-breaking quote that I have for you or something I did to stop the reality that my family was getting turned upside down. Sorry to give the news, but there may be seasons like this that shatter you, that are not glamorous or postworthy, that try to take your fight, that you do not understand. Seasons that words cannot seem to fix and where time seems to stand still.

The good news is you do not have to find under-standing. You do not have to make sense of it or control it. Proverbs 3:5–6 says, "Trust in the Lord with all your heart and lean not on your own understanding; in all your ways submit to him, and he will make your paths straight." You have a God that tells you to lean on Him, one that can withstand your full weight. A God that does not run and hide when things get tough but gets down in the mud with you. He does not have to be seen to show up for you. He does not have to be seen to be present in your storm. His love chases after you. His love casts out all fear! Even fear of the unknown. Even the fear of the how-can-I or the fear of the what-ifs.

I will recall all the days of my life the ways that God was there in that storm. I might have been blind to His ways in that season, but that does not mean God was blind to my storm. He was working on my family's behalf. He was there even when I was ungrateful and angry. In the hospital. In the surgery room. In the quiet of the night. When the tears flowed, when anger screamed, when there were no words. He was with us. He had the final say.

In Genesis 16:13 (CSB), we see Hagar use the name El Roi, which means "the God who sees us." I have found that to be true. He is El Roi in every season. He sees you right where you are. Let that comfort you. You can put your full weight on Him. Trust Him to support you through the crushing moments.

In the Scripture, we also see Jesus and Paul refer to God as Abba Father. This name tells us of God's fatherly nature, one that gives us covering and fights for us, one that can be trusted and leaned on, one that cares about what we care about and wants the best for us. Find comfort in His name.

Be strong and courageous. Do not be afraid; do not be discouraged, for the Lord your God will be with you wherever you go.
—Joshua 1:9

PRAYER:

Lord, I am going to be honest and real with you. I cannot see the way right now. I cannot see how I am going to make it past this mountain or how I will get past these waves that look like they will crash over me at any moment. So right now I read your words over my life, that *you* go with me wherever I go. When I am alone, you are there; when I doubt myself, you are there; when it is too much to bear, you are there. Thank you for not being afraid of my mess. Thank you that you are not scared away by my brokenness. I speak your words over my situation. You are my refuge. You are aware of what is going on. El Roi, you see me. Abba Father, you care for me. Right now I am unsure of a lot, but I am sure that I can hide under your wings. You say you are close to the brokenhearted and those crushed in spirit. Comfort me, Lord. Console me, Lord. In Jesus's name, amen.

CHAPTER 3

DOWN THE RABBIT HOLE

I never quite understood the Disney character of Alice. I did not understand why she was running around through the forest, persistent to catch up to a rabbit. How she jumped about scrambling, pushing to find him in her pretty blue dress. Finally catching up to him, only to discover a hole, dark and dirty, she continued to crawl into it. Not knowing what lay in the depths of this darkness, she continued to pursue the rabbit. What did she expect? Forward she crawled anyway until down, down, down she fell, landing in a world far away where nothing was real, crashing into what seemed to be a mesmerizing land of dreams—or her land of nightmares.

I felt like Alice falling, heading deeper into what I knew could not be good but welcoming it anyway, spiraling downhill into my depression, down into avoidance, down into the voices in my head that were louder than those outside. I was eighteen when I was deep in my hole, when that giant monster would reappear and follow me around. I was filling myself with things of the world, doing anything to just numb the overwhelming emotions. I turned to boys, parties, alcohol, dabbled in some drugs, all with the intention of giving my mind momentary escapes from my toxic thoughts.

My family had a lot going on, so I could easily slip under the radar, easily get lost, crawl into my dark and bottomless rabbit hole, not knowing what I might crash into, all while keeping my appearances fine tuned on the outside. But I was silently screaming on the inside, slipping away into my very own land of nightmares.

One night I found myself at this party full of zombies back before zombies were cool. Like Alice, I continued to crawl into the dark space. I was there to find Steven— yes, that one from years ago. I did not learn my lesson at that skating rink—I still thought he was going to be it. Through the years of middle and high school, I always stayed close to him. We were best friends, causing trouble around the town. I was secretly hoping that he would realize I was the one for him, but I did not mind the wait.

There he was leaning back on the wall, observing the crowd, just too cool for school. Maybe this would be the night he would finally see me, see how much I cared. I walked up to him, going over what I had been rehearsing. Some sentences came out. It was like they went right through him, hitting the wall behind him with a thud. He was looking at me but more like through me. I guess he was on one too many pills; I had seen him like this before. There was going to be no talking to him. His eyes looked so scary, hollow, numb, gone.

Over the edge I went, dropping into the dark. Next thing I knew, a fight broke out like always, cops arrived, and kids fled in every direction.

I found myself alone on the street, walking deeper into the night. I took a bottle from the party, got in my car, and went home. I don't remember much after that. But the details I do remember are vivid and full of overwhelming emotions. My thoughts were full of lies. I stopped fighting them and gave in. Down the rabbit hole I continued. The loudest of them all was, *I don't want to do this anymore.* I simply was done, exhausted with the battle that was going on within. I wanted the pain in my heart to stop. Who would notice if this quiet, dark night swallowed me up? Nothingness would be so much easier than this mess that existed inside.

I proceeded to plan what I thought would be the last night of my life. I planned the music, the place, down to the last outfit. I tiptoed to my room, past my snoring father on the couch, with pills and alcohol in hand, looking back to take one last glimpse of him. Down the hatch the pills went, until all five hundred disappeared.

The part I did not plan was waking up. It was far more difficult than swallowing pills. When I opened my eyes, the dread took its place. *No, no, no, no…how could this be?* Waking up to pain, bright lights, and concerned faces. Waking up to shame and guilt. I remember my grandmother patting my arm. I remember her saying, "I love you," words that had never come out of her mouth before.

From the hospital bed, I was transported to an institution. I avoided everyone's eyes, ashamed of the way I gave up on myself. Scared and isolated, I felt like a failure and weaker than ever. Luckily, I had already learned from many counselor sessions how to say exactly what the doctors wanted to hear, so I got out pretty quickly.

The sad thing is what they wanted to hear and what they said that made me build walls higher and go further into hiding. "See you soon. You will be back, girls like you always are," the counselor that checked me out of the institution said with a chuckle. His voice echoed in my head the whole car ride home. There I was greeted by my family and yet another counselor, all sitting in a circle with letters of what they wanted to say to me.

After they all got done reading their painful points of view, the counselor got his turn. "You see how selfish your decision was."

I, however, did not get a turn to speak but sat there stunned and silent. "Sorry," was all I could mumble. What could I possibly say that they would want to hear? They didn't want the truth. The truth that I was upset that I was not successful. The truth that I could not swallow the shame and guilt that were thrown around unintentionally in that circle. The truth that my thoughts wanted me dead.

Showers became my safe place where I could cry without being heard, where I could crumble, where I would attempt to clean away my guilt. Where I could take off the face that had it all under control and unmask the one that was overwhelmed. Overwhelmed with the urge to be strong, to fight the voices in my head telling me to give up.

To be transparent with you, attempting suicide and not succeeding at first did not give me a wake-up call. It did not make depression go away. In many ways, it only grew worse. I was hurting. I felt fragile, as if one gust of wind would break me and send me shattering across the floor.

Sometimes hurting is the first part of the healing. I wanted to be fixed but could not shake the feeling of being broken beyond repair. One thing I did know was I was going to prove those "counselors" wrong. I was not going back to that place, and I was not going to be another statistic. Depression was not going to win. I refused to take medication; I could do this on my own, or so I thought.

Sometimes hurting is the first part of the healing.

I was going to put up a fight, battle for my family, fight to actually want to live again. I wasn't sure how, but I was going to make my head better. In some tiny way, I knew deep down that if I fought hard enough one day, I could maybe help another little broken and lost girl. I held on to the tiny slice of hope that maybe, just maybe, one day the battle in my mind would not be so darn hard.

It was from this place that I struggled for quite some time, that I would battle to want to live again. It was not until my mother took me to church two months later that I began to ask myself different questions. My questions now were: How could Jesus use me? I tried to take my life.

Didn't that put me down in some book of the untouchable? Wasn't He mad at me for taking what He gave me, my very breath, for granted? How could He love me and fight for me when for months I just wanted to throw in the towel? But I made a daily decision: who I have been does not have to dictate who I can become because it is not what I go through that determines where I end up, it is my perspective along the way.

When I look back on this season of my life, it quite often still brings me to my knees with thankfulness. If it had not been for God on my side, I would not be standing. I am not here today because I didn't give up on God—I am here today because God did not give up on me. I can hardly wrap my brain around it. It was the greatest demonstration of love I have ever witnessed. I did not see God, but He still saw me. I did not seek Him out, but He came to my rescue. I was doing all the wrong things, but He still saved me. God saw something in me that I had yet to see in myself: value. He loved me back then just as much as He loves me right now. This was a very important lesson that I would continually learn: God chose me long before I chose Him, and God's love is not earned—nothing I do can make Him take it away.

He loves you despite you. He made you knowing all your darkest moments so far and all the ones still to come. Nothing can change God's love for you; nothing can take it away. Not what they did to you. Not what you did to yourself. Not what keeps you up at night or what breaks your heart. Not even death can separate you from the love of God in Christ Jesus (Rom. 8:38–39). There is no such thing as untouchable for God. Just look anywhere in the Bible.

Jesus touched the diseased and healed them, turned Christian-killers into disciples, raised the dead to life, parted seas, sent plagues to set His people free, showed prostitutes compassion and love, spoke up for those that could not speak, sent angels to help when one was suicidal, and turned the lame into walking and the blind into seeing. There is nothing that can disqualify you from His love. It was a love that was never earned, yet it is poured out for each one of us. And it was from these truths where I would learn about His grace.

Who I have been does not dictate who I can become.

Before we dive into that, I want to give you a few reminders of what God, the creator of heaven and earth, says concerning you. Yeah, you read correctly, you. That mighty and massive God, the one who holds the stars and can part the sea, is the same one who is concerned with you. He is the same God who collects your tears and knows the number of hairs on your head. He cares about you. He has written His words down for you to remember if you find yourself in this place of crushing. Here are just a few things to remember and to speak out over your circumstances. Speak out over that darkness, and watch it flee.

- God says, "I will be with you" (Isa. 43:2).

- God says, "I will deliver you" (Ps. 50:15).

- God says, "I will teach you" (Ps. 32:8).

- God says, "I will listen to you" (Jer. 29:12).

- God says, "I will uphold you" (Isa. 41:10).

- God says, "I will give you the victory" (Ps. 44:6).

- God says, "I will show you mercy" (Eph. 2:4).

- God says, "I will put a new song in your mouth" (Ps. 40:2).

- God says, "I will strengthen you" (Exod. 15:2).

- God says, "I will direct you" (Ps. 42:8).

For I was so utterly burdened beyond my strength that I despaired of life itself. Indeed, I felt that I had received the sentence of death. But that was to make me rely not on myself but on God who raises the dead. He delivered me from such a deadly peril, and he will deliver me. On Him I have set my hope that he will deliver me again.
—2 Corinthians 1:8–10 (Personalized)

Maybe you find yourself in this place that I was, done, ready to give up, hopeless, consumed by darkness. Maybe it is not suicide but giving up on a dream or losing a relationship or a job or getting heartbroken. Whatever it is that you are losing hope in, please hear me. God sees you in this place. Let Him comfort you here. Call on Him. He will never turn His back on you, that I am certain of. There is nothing God cannot deliver you from. Depression, suicide, fear, anxiety, sickness—nothing stands a chance against the power of God. Exodus 14:14 says, "The LORD will fight for you; you need only to be still." With Him fighting for you, you cannot lose.

Suicide opened up my eyes to a reality where, from relationships to environments, I could look all over for something to fill the void I felt, but no one or no thing would ever fill it. And you definitely cannot drive out darkness with more darkness. No amount of alcohol or wild nights was going to cut it. It was a God-sized hole. That was what I was missing, what I was searching for: a relationship with my creator. Nothing else could take the place of that.

PRAYER:

Lord, the truth is I am outnumbered by the troubles around me. I don't even know where to begin to pray or what I would ask. I feel like I am disqualified and undeserving. Your word says that you can even see the cries of my heart. I need you, Lord. Thank you that you say you are close to me, that you never fail me. I turn to you in all my ways. I hide in your wings; you are my refuge. I ask that you help me to remember what you say about me, that you replace the toxic things in my head with your beautiful and powerful truths. I give you the authority over all my heart and mind. Shine light on all the darkness, and make it flee! Help me to see your love. Help me to see you. In Jesus's name, amen.

CHAPTER 4

IT'S A SETUP

I am going to come clean. I am a romantic. I could sit and read poetry for hours on end, which I am sure you have guessed by now. I love the build-ups, the plot twist, the love-conquers-all stories and happy endings. But would a memorable romance story be great without conflict? No, it would not. Without conflict, there is no character development. If there is no character development, there is no lesson. With no lesson, there is no learning.

This brings me to a reality that I have learned: there is a purpose for your pain.

Let me take that even further. Every limitation, every affliction, every tear you've cried, every broken heart, they all serve a purpose. Every conflict you are in, like it or not, is developing you. God might not have done it to you, but He sure will get the glory from it. It is written in Scripture that all things—not some things, not just the pretty things—but all things work together for good to those that love God (Rom. 8:28).

I want to spend some time dissecting the scripture below. Full disclosure: I am not a Bible scholar, although

I do believe from the bottom of my heart that the Bible is living and breathing, that it speaks to every person in a different way. You just have to have the ears to listen. So this is how it spoke to me.

Because of the extravagance of those revelations, and so I wouldn't get a big head, I was given the gift of a handicap to keep me in constant touch with my limitations. Satan's angel did his best to get me down; what he in fact did was push me to my knees. No danger then of walking around high and mighty! At first I didn't think of it as a gift, and begged God to remove it. Three times I did that, and then he told me, My grace is enough; it's all you need. My strength comes into its own in your weakness.

Once I heard that, I was glad to let it happen. I quit focusing on the handicap and began appreciating the gift. It was a case of Christ's strength moving in on my weakness. Now I take limitations in stride, and with good cheer, these limitations that cut me down to size—abuse, accidents, opposition, bad breaks. I just let Christ take over! And so the weaker I get, the stronger I become.
—2 Corinthians 12:7–10 (MSG)

I can almost be certain that we can all relate to this. Every single one of us has some type of thorn. What is yours? What is pushing you down no matter what you do? The thing that is tormenting you. The thing that is trying to take your joy, your peace, your contentment. Every time you try to move on or take a step, it is right there, reminding you, digging into your side, trying to make you collapse, trying to bring you to your knees, trying to stop you in your tracks, trying to keep you from moving forward. You can try to run. You can try to ignore it, but nothing will numb it for long. It is always there causing you suffering.

The even harder question to answer is what do you do when you ask God to take it away from you and get the answer "I am enough"? What do you do when you realize this might take a perspective change?

You are not alone in this. You are not the only one going through suffering—that is just what the enemy wants you to think. Jesus even went through this. In the garden, He cried out to His father three times, asking Him to take the bitter cup that He was about to receive. He was so overwhelmed that He was sweating blood from every pore in His body. He who committed no sin was put to a brutal death for you and me so that we can live in freedom. He wanted to give up in the garden. He asked if He could do it any other way. And yet He still chose to do God's will.

Jesus had the insight that went far beyond the garden that the pain he was going to go through served a great purpose, a purpose we are still reaping benefits from today. What if the cup passed from Him in that garden? What if He said, "Okay, Father, I toss in the towel, just get me out of here"? Thank God we will never know what would've happened if Jesus did not go to the cross for us!

Here I was left with this thorn of depression, a gift from the enemy. For me, it wasn't a person—it came in the form of a voice in my head. Side note: a person is not your thorn; do not give them that much power. The Bible says we do not battle with things of this world but things of the spirit (Eph. 6:12). The greatest Goliaths are not your crazy coworkers, horrible exes, or the mean girls at school. Many of our biggest obstacles stare at us in the mirror. The most immobilizing afflictions are the ones not seen. The ones that are silent and replayed in your mind daily. The ones that come out when the people leave, the makeup comes off, and you are all alone.

Heather, you're selfish, how could you have done that? Heather, you are weak, you gave up on yourself. You let darkness win. Heather, you couldn't even kill yourself.

Thoughts raced around in my head, but I still managed a smile as the counselor assured me I was making great progress. They believed that I had come a long way. I begged God to take this from me. I wanted to be better! I did not want to think like this anymore. These thoughts had got to go. But they did not go.

What do you do when it doesn't go away? What do you do when it is trying to cripple you? One of the difficult things about a thorn is it comes with you everywhere. It is not this thing you can just choose to take out and save for later. It comes to work. It comes to the party. It even comes to church. You could be sitting there trying to worship, trying to focus, but there it is right in your side, this painful distraction.

When I was studying this scripture, the Lord's reply really made me think. He simply said, "My grace is enough for you."

Would you be okay with this response? I was not. I was so caught up in my issue I was blind to see how God wanted to use it, blind to see how any good could come from this. "God, I am hurting! I can't get past this, Lord! Are you even there? Do you even care about me?"

"My grace is enough."

"But what does that *mean?*"

If we look back in the scripture after the Lord answered him, Paul's words and attitude change immediately.

Once I heard that, I was glad to let it happen. I quit focusing on the handicap and began appreciating the gift.

—2 Corinthians 12:9 (MSG)

That means this grace thing must be something way more important than what I understood it to be. It had to be more than just these scriptures we can all quote on Instagram, a saying I can loosely throw around. If this grace thing helped Paul and completely changed his perspective about his pain, then I wanted it too.

God does not lie to us. He does not say things just to make us feel better. He knows the power behind words. He speaks the truth. If He said His grace is sufficient for what we are going through, then it is. So let's take a deeper look at it.

What Does It Mean?

Grace is God's kindness or favor on you. Grace in Greek means "charis" or favor. Grace in Hebrew means "to bend or stoop in kindness." Picture God stooping down to you in your mess, in your pain, in your brokenness. In His unmerited kindness, He reaches you in your need and places upon you favor. It is quite beautiful. It is a beautiful expression of His compassion toward you. So how do you get it?

Grace Is Unearned
For it is by grace [charis] you have been saved, through faith—and this is not from yourselves, it is the gift of God—not by works, so that no one can boast. For we are God's handiwork, created in Christ Jesus to do good works, which God prepared in advance for us to do.
　—Ephesians 2:8–10

You can't earn this. It is not by your works or this "do-good" checklist you made up. You do not get grace by behavior modification. No one can take it away from you because no one gave it to you—it is a gift from God. There is no checklist you can create to get the grace of God; it is simply placed on you when you give your life to Him. The gift of eternal salvation is linked to God's grace.

Grace Is Undeserved
I definitely did not deserve God's grace when I tried to take my life. I was literally running in the opposite direction of Him. And yet He still reached down into my problem and poured His grace out on me.

You know what really hurts my heart is when I hear people say, "I will start going to church when I get it together. I will give my life to God when I stop doing this and that." They are missing out on a relationship with God right now because for some reason they think God wants perfection. Sorry to break it to you, but we can never reach perfection. Philippians 3:14 says we press on to obtain the goal, we move forward and give it our best, and Jesus comes in and fills the gaps. I was so scared to step into church knowing all my sins and my past.

But my past never disqualified me from His saving grace because I never qualified for it in the first place. Our Heavenly Father has already taken into consideration all of our stupid mistakes and said, "My grace is still enough for that."

Jesus says, "Oh, you are weak? Perfect, I do my best work in weakness."

Look at Paul! He was murdering Christians, on his way to take some more out, and God met him there on the road to Damascus (Acts 9). He showed him grace, radically changing the trajectory of his life forever. He went from brutally opposing Christians to being the author of most of the New Testament!

Grace Is Unlimited

John 1:16 (ESV) says, "For from his fullness we have all received, grace upon grace." There is enough to go around. God is not there on His throne saying, "Heather, girl, you really messed up this week. Your grace is running low. I would definitely lay low for the rest of the week. You wouldn't want to run out." No! Scripture says grace upon grace! It is sufficient for everything you are going through every single day. Every day you have the grace of God stooping down to reach into your situation.

Grace is unearned. You didn't earn it, and it can't be taken from you.
Grace is undeserved. It is a gift from God.
Grace is unlimited. It never runs out.

Grace is the answer. We want to grow in grace. "But grow in the grace and knowledge of our Lord and Savior Jesus Christ. To him be glory both now and forever! Amen" (2 Pet. 3:18, ESV). Grow in grace by growing in your relationship with Christ. We need to shift our perspective, like Paul did. Stop focusing on the affliction, and start surrendering it over to God. The weaker we are, the stronger He is in us! The more we humbly surrender, the stronger we get.

I am glad that depression pushed me to my knees. If God did not allow the thorn, how could I see His grace? If I did not experience sorrow, how could I appreciate joy? If I didn't experience brokenness, how could I understand what it felt like to be whole? If the enemy did not knock me to my knees, how could Jesus pick me back up? I am glad it happened because it helped me learn about the love of God and His grace upon grace.

Through my suicide attempt and struggle with depression, I was just getting knocked into position. You see, it led to my mom taking me to church about two months after my attempt. I walked in there with some thorns, but when I heard about Jesus, I knew that He had a purpose for my life because His grace saved me. I knew in my heart that He saved me that night, that I should have died from overdosing.

I was not sure about much, but I knew I could not hang around the same crowds anymore. I knew I could not party away my problems. I knew I needed to know more about this man named Jesus and the love He had for me. There was no escaping the fact that what I had been searching for was a relationship with Christ Jesus. So I just let Christ take over. I gave my life to him and never turned back. The whole time I was begging God to take away this depression, it was the very thing He was using to position me.

Your history does not have to determine your future. Your very misery can become your ministry, just like the apostle Paul turned his prison into a pulpit.

What are you praying for God to take away? What if what you are asking Him to take away is the very thing He wants to use to bless you with? What if what you see as a thorn God sees as a way to get closer to you? What if what you see as pain God sees as a way to strengthen you? What if what you see as an affliction God sees as a way to draw near to you?

What area do you need the grace of God in? I dare you to boldly stop asking Him to take it away and instead start asking Him for His grace and His strength to come in and make you strong in your weakness. He is so full of love and mercy that He reaches into our pit and scoops us out and sets our feet on solid ground.

You might be walking with a limp, but God calls you victorious.

You might have some scars, but God calls you beautifully made.

You might have a past, but God calls you by a new name.

You might feel alone, but God calls you His friend.

You might feel like a failure, but God calls you chosen.

I am not sure what you are walking around with, but I do know that God will use it in some way for good. Instead of asking Him to take it away, pray for the strength to endure, to push forward, to use it to help someone down the road.

Your misery can become your ministry.

I know that this is counterculture. We want to feel good; we do not want to feel pain. Do not let the momentary affliction blind you from your eternal mind-set, for this is a mere moment, and it serves a purpose. God has made *everything* beautiful in the correct timing. "He has made everything beautiful in its time. He has also set eternity in the human heart; yet no one can fathom what God has done from beginning to end" (Eccles. 3:11).

I can imagine that Paul did not feel like he had God's favor when he was knocked off his horse and blinded for three days (Acts 9). The Israelites probably did not feel favored as the Egyptians closed in and the Red Sea was in front of them (Exod. 14). Joseph might not have felt like God was for him as he was thrown in a pit to die by his own brothers (Gen. 37). But each one saw the favor of God at the right time. Paul would become one of the most influential leaders of the early church. Moses reached out his staff, the Red Sea parted, and all the Egyptians were swallowed up by the waters. Joseph would later be lord over the land, just like in his dreams.

It is a setup. God's grace is enough for what you are going through. Let us pray for help to switch our perspective, just like Paul.

PRAYER:

Heavenly Father, I know that you are a good God, a faithful God, my strength and my provider. Thank you for seeing me in this affliction. You see what I am struggling with. Thank you for Your grace that swoops into my pain. Thank you that your favor is upon me. I ask that you help me to see this thorn like you see it. Help me to see past the momentary pain to the eternal purpose. I ask that your will be done in my life. Help me to learn and grow in grace. Help me one day at a time. Pour your peace out that surpasses all understanding. I give my weakness over to you. Thank you for your unfailing love. In Jesus's name, amen.

CHAPTER 5

UPSIDE DOWN OR RIGHT-SIDE UP?

Foundations. We all have one, either created by family or the environments around us. The thing about them is that you never know how sturdy yours is until it is truly tested, until it is shaken, cracked open, or even pulled out from under you.

I often found myself trying to stand on anything that looked like it would hold my full weight, leaping from brick to brick, expecting this one to not give way like the last one. I quickly learned they were not going to support me for long.

When you choose to follow Jesus and give your life to Him, it is a beautiful, life-changing moment. It is the best decision that you will ever make. Although I had made that decision to submit my all to Him, to stop running and instead pursue the one chasing after me, it was not all rainbows and butterflies. No one had ever told me what was to come next: rebuilding. I guess it does not really preach well. And to some it might seem to be common sense. But is there really such a thing as common sense?

You could say traffic lights are common sense. Red means stop. Green means go. Yellow means speed up—I mean slow down. But if your town never had a traffic light, it would not be common sense to you. It would take adjustment. It would take time to learn about the lights.

There should totally be a crash course for newbie Christians. People should tell you that church is like a hospital for broken people. That Christians are not perfect. That pastors are still human. That the enemy still comes like a flood. That your "holy high" can come crashing down the moment you step into the parking lot, and that a saved person will beep impatiently at you using some not-so-biblical words. That Christianity is uncomfortable. That the cost to follow Jesus is high.

As God was becoming my new foundation, my old one was falling away. And it was not such a good feeling. It can feel as if your world is falling apart. It can be very confusing. Friends fade away, even your very best ones. Family can think you are weird. People still want you to be the old you; they tell you that you are becoming too different, that you are not the same person you used to be.

The creation of new habits is not always comfortable. I now wanted to be at church on Sundays. I knew that to be serious about this life I needed to dive in, no testing the waters here. I would sign up for every event or volunteer opportunity I could. My family asked if I was part of a cult. I felt like I was slowly becoming the black sheep, not fitting in where I used to but not fitting in with the new church crowd either. I felt stuck in this strange in-between.

Please hear me correctly. I am not saying that I said yes to God and then stopped every bad thing I was doing. That is not true. I still fell to sin constantly. But now I had this thing in my stomach that tried to stop me, warn me, guide me, this thing I could not just push away anymore, the Holy Spirit.

I just wanted somewhere to fit in. It was easy to fall into old ways. Those were the foundations that were built into me. I felt so frustrated for a while. And to be honest, I wanted to give up a lot. I thought following Jesus would be so much easier than this. That people would be as excited as I was. I thought that trouble would magically avoid me.

It was like this old me was clinging on, trying to come back up because at least I fit in there. I could hide there. It was comfortable. But the new me wanted to break through! I could not walk in true freedom with my old chains dragging behind, and it seems Paul felt this way too.

For I have the desire to do what is good, but I cannot carry it out. For I do not do the good I want to do, but the evil I do not want to do—this I keep on doing...but I see another law at work in me, waging war against the law of my mind...What a wretched man I am!
—Romans 7:18, 23–24

There was a war waging in my mind to cling to the old and to push into the new me all at the same time.

Once I understood I was not alone in this struggle, it helped me greatly. If you are having a hard time with this, I want to encourage you today. If you feel like you just cannot fit in, do not be disheartened. If you feel like your world is shaking, have courage. If friends and family are turning away from you, take heart. If you had different expectations of this walk with Christ, it's time to lay them down. He has far more than you could ever think or imagine in store for you. It is in these moments that God is doing amazing things. You are not called to fit in. Quite the opposite, actually. You are called to be set apart, the light in the dark. There is nothing normal about following God. All throughout Scripture we see "normal" being thrown out. We see many valleys and mountains, we see wars and peace, we see love and chaos in the lives of the disciples.

If your world is shaking, maybe God is getting rid of some things that were weighing you down. Maybe your environment is trembling because you are shedding off some things. Your life could be shifting because God could be taking you to a new level. Some people will not make it to the next level with you. Some behaviors might have to go before you can be elevated. It is time to let go of those faulty foundations and let God have way in your heart. It might seem like your world is getting turned upside down, but maybe it is just turning right-side up.

Here I was, this broken, suicidal Christian newbie, crying out to God, praying earnestly, "I want to be more like you, Jesus." I was desperate for God to help me, pleading for Him to fix my heart and help my mind, not fully understanding what I was asking. 2 Corinthians 5:17 (NLT) says, "This means that anyone who belongs to Christ has become a new person. The old life is gone; a new life has begun!" No wonder I felt like everything was getting turned upside down. That time of pain, confusion, and breaking was me becoming a new person in Christ. I was not fitting in anymore because I was made new.

Then Jesus told his disciples, "If anyone would come after me, let him deny himself and take up his cross and follow me. For whoever would save his life will lose it, but whoever loses his life for my sake will find it. For what will it profit a man if he gains the whole world and forfeits his soul? Or what shall a man give in return for his soul?"
Matthew 16:24–26

You might have heard this scripture before about picking up your cross. I did not understand the concept at the time. Praying to be more like Jesus is not some light prayer. Following Jesus is not this bumper sticker quote or a way to escape trouble. Jesus was crucified, tortured, mocked, an outcast, forsaken by His dearest friends, and betrayed by those He loved. He turned the whole world on its head in a few short years. He shattered the norm. His story is the most influential one to ever hit bookstores, transforming lives forevermore. And we pray, "Lord, make me more like you."

"If anyone would come after me, let him deny himself and take up his cross and follow me" (Matt. 16:24). This is one dangerous prayer that could shake up your norm. It is not to be taken lightly.

"For whoever would save his life will lose it, but whoever loses his life for my sake will find it" (Matt. 16:25). This walk, at times, can feel like death. We put our flesh to death daily. This might sound extreme, but if you have been through it, you know the pain of the process. It hurts on the inside. It can leave you doubled over. It can leave you confused, wanting to retreat. You may not be able to explain it, but that does not take away the fact of its realness.

Do not be blindsided. We love to read that we receive the life of Jesus but do not pay much attention to the rest of the verse…and His death. It is written we must lose our life to gain it in Christ. Do not let the enemy lie to you and tempt you to give up or to go back, that you cannot do it or that you are too weak, that it is just too hard, so this must not be God. This is part of the walk. Death is part of life. Not the glamorous one. Not the Instagram-posting, Facebook-sharing life. But it nonetheless is a part.

Although it might take your breath away at times, it will not consume you. Although the storm might be raging, it will not overtake you. Jesus came down as a man and went through all these things for you and me. There is nothing that you are dealing with that He cannot help you through.

So what do you do when you are facing death of your wants and desires, death of what you thought it was going to look like, death of dreams, death of friends or family, death of the old you, death of your flesh? How do you push past this feeling?

There is no easy answer, but there is a way. You let go. You fix your focus on Jesus. You step out in faith. Each day, regardless of what gets thrown your way, you make the decision to put your trust in your creator. What does this look like? How can we do this? Let's look at this story of Peter.

As soon as the meal was finished, he insisted that the disciples get in the boat and go on ahead to the other side while he dismissed the people.

Meanwhile, the boat was far out to sea when the wind came up against them and they were battered by the waves. At about four o'clock in the morning, Jesus came toward them walking on the water. They were scared out of their wits. "A ghost!" they said, crying out in terror.

But Jesus was quick to comfort them. "Courage, it's me. Don't be afraid."

Peter, suddenly bold, said, "Master, if it's really you, call me to come to you on the water."

He said, "Come ahead."

Jumping out of the boat, Peter walked on the water to Jesus. But when he looked down at the waves churning beneath his feet, he lost his nerve and started to sink. He cried, "Master, save me!"

Jesus didn't hesitate. He reached down and grabbed his hand.

—Matthew 14:22, 24–31 (MSG)

Let Go of Your Plan

The first thing to take from this is Jesus sends them into the waters—and into the storm. God had a plan. He knew it was going to storm. He knew that Jesus was going to perform the miracle of walking on the water. "'For my thoughts are not your thoughts, neither are your ways my ways,' declares the Lord. 'As the heavens are higher than the earth, so are my ways higher than your ways and my thoughts than your thoughts'" (Isa. 55:8–9).

If Jesus told the disciples that it was going to storm badly, do you think they would've been reluctant to get in the boat? What if He told them, "Do not worry, I will walk on to the water to you"? Do you think they would've laughed and not believed Him? When Jesus told Peter what He had to do on the cross, Peter tried to talk Him out of it. There is a reason that things are not revealed to us all at once. Scripture says in Psalm 119:105 that "God's words are a lamp to our feet, a light on the path." A lamp, not an LED stadium light.

Jesus can send you into a messy place. He may send you somewhere that does not make sense. He may even send you somewhere that seems to be opposite of your calling. You may be obeying Jesus, only for a storm to hit. You may be following what He has put on your heart, only for you to lose the job. You may be obeying Him, only for the relationship to end or them to leave you. And you are left in the middle of the waves, looking around, confused, overwhelmed, or downright angry, thinking to yourself, *Did I miss something?* This is the time to trust. If Jesus sent you out into it, He has a plan. He can see the end and everything in between. What if the storm is the very thing He wants to use to perform a miracle in your life?

You have to let go of your way. We must let go of our plan. We cannot come to God with our agenda and our blueprints and expect Him to do it point by point. What kind of relationship is that? How would that be trusting God? This is not a business deal. It is a relationship. God is not our genie in a bottle. His ways are not our ways. His thoughts are not our thoughts. His ways are higher. He sees the beginning, the end, and the bumps on the way.

Simply trust. Trust that He has a plan, one that will blow your mind, a plan that you cannot even fathom. You might simply want to get to the other side safe from the storm, but He might want you to walk over the storm on the water. You might want to simply be stable and have a good job, but He wants you to have influence in His kingdom. You might want a house and a family, but He might want you to have a thriving ministry worldwide. I encourage you to stop asking Him to bless your plan and start asking for His agenda to unfold in your life.

Stop asking Him to bless your plan, and start asking for His agenda to unfold in your life.

Fix Your Focus on Jesus

But Jesus was quick to comfort them. "Courage, it's me. Don't be afraid."

Peter, suddenly bold, said, "Master, if it's really you, call me to come to you on the water."

He said, "Come ahead."

Jumping out of the boat, Peter walked on the water to Jesus.

—Matthew 14:27–28 (MSG)

Notice that Jesus did not stop the waves or the storm, which He could have. Instead He said, "Come to me in the middle of it." There is no storm, no wave, no obstacle that you do not have the authority in Jesus's name to walk on. Jesus is above all things. He did not stop the waves but kept Peter above them. Peter jumped out in faith and was successful at walking on the water!

The storm doesn't always have to stop for you to have peace in it. The things going on around you do not have to change for you to find joy. As long as your focus is on Jesus, nothing will overcome you. He is our anchor, our fortress, an ever-present help in times of trouble.

The storm doesn't always have to stop for you to have peace in it.

The environment around you might crumble, but we stand on the word of God that is immovable. He wants to keep you safe in the midst of the mess.

Peter was successfully doing what Jesus was calling him to despite what was going on around him—until he lost his focus. Peter's faith wavered when he realized what he was doing. This can get us caught up.

Just because the storm has not stopped does not mean you are going in the wrong direction. John 16:33 (ESV) says, "I have said these things to you that in me you may have peace. In the world you *will* have tribulation. But take heart: I have overcome the world [emphasis mine]." Scripture makes it plain that it is not always easy. It shows us there will be some hurdles. But take heart because Jesus is right there with you.

Do not get distracted because it's hard. Do not get disheartened because it's taking so much more effort than you thought. As long as your focus is on Jesus, the storm will not overcome you. Lock onto Him. Push into His presence. Seek and He will be found. He is never far from you. Once you start turning from Him and looking at the waves, it is a wrap, so stay focused on moving forward, maintaining in faith even when in the middle of storms by keeping your eyes on Jesus's power rather than your inadequacies.

Step Out in Faith
It takes courage to step out in faith. Faith is so important to our walk with Jesus, and we will cover it more in depth in chapters to come. Imagine jumping out of the boat in the middle of an intense storm and walking toward Jesus. I am sure the first few steps were adrenaline pumping and thrilling. Then a crack of lightning in the distance or maybe a deep rumbling of thunder or the glimpse of

a swell forming in the distance caught the attention of Peter, and all that courage left. He began looking back at the boat, at his friends still there staring at him, at the deep, dark water under his feet. He must have thought, *What was I thinking?* Then he began to go under.

This can happen more often than I would like to admit. Actually, just the other day I was trying to learn how to surf. Even though I am currently in Australia, where obviously all the *Shark Week* clips come from, I get all excited when I see the waves. They look absolutely stunning when I am standing ankle deep as a bystander.

So I boldly ran into the water, paddled out, and sat on the board, feet dangling in the water. Then I took my eyes off the goal and started looking at the still, deep water that my feet were in. Fear flooded in. Good old *Jaws* went off in my head; that darn theme song played. Next thing I knew, I was paddling frantically back to shore as if my life depended on it.

Take something more serious. God called me to leave my job, my home, my family, to pack up and hit the road. California, here I come. I had courage, and my faith was strong. As I said bye to my family, I jumped in my Jeep and hit the road. I was thrilled to be following the call, chasing what God put in my heart regardless of the cost. Then I looked back into the rearview mirror. My town was now getting farther and farther away. When I took my eyes off what was ahead and kept looking back, my faith seemed to be choked out by my doubt, and fear of the unknown came in like a flood.

But when he looked down at the waves churning beneath his feet, he lost his nerve and started to sink. He cried, "Master, save me!"

Jesus didn't hesitate. He reached down and grabbed his hand.

—Matthew 14:30–31 (MSG)

Faith often calls us out to the deep, away from the shore, away from others, away from our safety nets. The moment we lose our focus, we sink. When we start to look out at our problems, doubt floods our mind. Fear chokes out our faith like a weed. In one moment, the promise that Jesus made can seem so far away. But that is not the truth—that is a lie because the word says Jesus immediately reached out for Peter with no hesitation. Jesus might call you into the deep away from others but never away from Him.

He is not standing there, arms crossed, watching you sink, annoyed that you lost your focus, saying, "You should have had more faith." Jesus is right there an arm's length away from you, ready to reach in and grab you. All it takes is three words: "Jesus, save me."

Do not be discouraged if you are here. You stepped out in faith, and you lost your focus. Now you are sinking, desperate for rescue. It takes one call. Just ask Jesus to save you. When you utter His name, the enemy must flee. There is power in His name. Chains break in His name. There is strength in surrender. We do not always need the answers. We do not always need to know the end. We just need Jesus. We just need His word to be a lamp to our feet, one step at a time. When you speak His name, He reaches into your situation, embraces you with compassion and love, and corrects you with His wisdom. He is the answer.

So if you are feeling stuck, confused about this walk, lost in the waves, overwhelmed by the storm, experiencing the death of your dreams or the death of your flesh, or your foundations are getting rebuilt—remember His ways are not going to match yours. Stay focused on Jesus and the promises. Keep stepping out in faith one foot at a time.

Let go of your plan. His plan is way better.

Fix your focus on Jesus. He is with you in the storm.

Step out in faith. He is your courage.

PRAYER:

Heavenly Father, thank you that you are good. That you want the best for me. The truth is I need you. I have been holding on to my plans and my way for too long. I surrender over my agenda to you. I ask that you have your way in my life in every single area. I do not want to do anything without you in it. I ask when I lose my focus that you will remind me to remain fixed on you. When I get scared, I pray you calm me with your peace. I ask when the waves look like they are going to take me out to remind my spirit that you are right there with me, walking me over them. Thank you that you are in every season. Thank you that you never leave my side. I love you. In Jesus's name, amen.

CHAPTER 6

TEAR DOWN THE WALL

My breathing was constricted, almost like there was a hand gripping my lungs—a hand that was not planning on releasing me any time soon. I was paralyzed by shock, every cell in my body trembling beyond control. My brain was going over every moment from the bar to the parking lot, going over the broken glass lying sprayed across the dirty sidewalk, going over every single detail to the moment that changed so much. The moment that now left me dazed and immobilized on the ground. Alone. Alone to get myself up. Alone to look for my keys that were thrown somewhere in the tall grass. Alone to deal with the deafening question of *what now?* Alone to the echo of the painful words that were lingering in the air.

I didn't know which direction to go. Who could console me? Whom could I share this with? But if I shared the series of unfortunate events, it would make them real, and I did not want them to be real. Not at all. If I drove to my apartment, he would most likely be there to greet me. If I drove to my parents', they would know something happened.

I coached myself to steady my shaking body, secretly hoping that he would come out of his apartment and apologize, scoop me off the floor into his arms, and tell me he was so sorry and that he just lost control. That it was not him, that he would never put his hands on me again, that he would ask me what he could do to make this better, how he could fix what he just broke, tell me that he would do anything.

But he did not come back out. He did not apologize. He did not take back the words or actions. *Get up, Heather.*

I was just trying to focus on the road, trying to stop the monsoon leaking from my eyes. "Just drive. You are okay. Focus. Breathe. Stop crying. You're fine," I coached myself out loud.

As I pulled up in my parents' driveway, I pulled down the mirror. "Who are you? How did you get here? Why did we avoid all the flags?"

I cleaned up my smeared makeup, wiped away the tears. I fixed my broken car console that had been a victim in the fight. With my big-girl face on, I tiptoed into my parents' house, got a blanket, and lay on the couch as if I could somehow sleep. Adrenaline was now leaving my body, and pain took its place. Pain in my back from hitting the ground. Pain in my legs spotted with dirt and grass. Tenderness in my ankles from where I was pulled out of the car.

What do I do from here? This was a new giant in front of me. No one had ever laid a hand on me with the intention to hurt me. Especially not someone I loved.

Jacob and I met in church in 2013. It was my first time volunteering when we met. He was everything I was not. He was confident, bold, life of the room. His joy and energy were contagious to anyone around him. I immediately thought that this could be the best relationship that I had ever been in. We both loved God, and we both served the church. We quickly jumped into a relationship neither one of us was ready to handle. I was not even sure what a godly relationship looked like, much less how to be in one.

In the beginning, there were many red flags we both ignored, and sin began to eat away at us. I came in with way too many past pains not healed yet, and he was not living the life he portrayed on the outside. We were on and off for over six years. The last two years were by far the hardest. They were the years of lies, abuse, and darkness.

I knew all the right "Christian sayings" and knew how to wear a smile to perfection. I knew how to keep up with the outward appearance, but inside I was crumbling with shame. I must admit that I was unable to sympathize with women that stayed with men that abused them—until I got a sip of it. Until I understood that it was not the physical abuse that paralyzed me but the mental. I felt crazy for a few weeks, like it was somehow one way or another my fault. Maybe if I didn't "set him off." Maybe it was because he was under a lot of stress in the season he was in. Stress from work, family, the church. *This is not him. I can help him change.*

I felt pathetic, worthless, and fake. Nothing was safe for me anymore, especially church, where I had to keep it all together with a pretty, little bow on top. Where I would have to sit across from him and smile as we led together. I was taking part in a massive facade. I needed a serious wake-up call. I built walls upon walls created in my heart. I felt broken beyond repair.

Somewhere past the walls I created, there was this faint truth I knew. I was not crazy. No matter what he said or did not say, this was real. No matter how drunk he was or wasn't, this was not right. No matter if he pretended it never happened, the moments replayed in my mind like a bad movie.

So what did I do? I went for help. I went to a Christian counselor I knew could be trusted with my truth.

She told me what I did not want to hear. She unloaded even more statements that I was hiding from myself. "This was only the beginning, Heather. Most, not all but most, cases get worse. But only you can make the decision to leave him, no matter what I say."

But I kept telling myself this was not him. He could change.

The best advice she gave me was for the next time it would happen. "Write it all down, and take pictures of the marks. That way when you try to ignore it or pretend it was not real, you cannot."

She was right. I think it was easier to pretend we were this couple doing good for God rather than a couple getting destroyed by sin, a couple that was losing to the monsters of anger, shame, and guilt. I knew that I had to face it, that I could not hide any longer. Our relationship had grown beyond toxic. I knew that if I wanted to be the best version of myself this had to be exposed.

Scripture says that the enemy is like a lion that comes to steal, kill, and destroy. Once Jacob and I gave him a foothold, he sure did that, leaving us both battered and scarred.

I share this story with you because I learned some vital lessons the hard way from this dark season in my life. I thought if I just left Jacob it would all go away. Time would ease the pain, right? One day it would not hurt so bad, right? I was not taking into consideration the damage that was done to my heart. I did not understand the magnitude of healing that needed to occur. Although I was moving forward, there was still this part in me that was stuck. I was not in pain anymore, but that pain just hardened into something else. I knew deep down I was not healed, just numb.

God revealed to me one Sunday that I had hate in my heart now instead of pain. It was like the pain of abuse turned into a nasty infection. I was living in offense. I hated him for breaking my heart in so many ways. And worse, I hated myself for allowing it to happen. I knew what I had to do: expose the hate to God.

I recall this one time when I was in high school, I was running around the neighborhood with some friends, causing havoc like normal. And of course I was barefoot while playing an intense game of manhunt. While running for dear life, I stepped on a piece of glass. Man, did it hurt! But I was not going to let it stop me—I would not lose! I did not want it to slow me down, so instead of looking at it and pulling it all out like a normal person, I quickly wiped my foot and continued to play. I just shifted my weight and pressed on through the pain. Eventually, my foot went numb, and I forgot it was in there.

I know what you are thinking, how did I forget a piece of glass was in my foot? I still ponder that. I even went to bed without treating it, foot still numb. When I woke up the next morning, the pain was unbearable. I went to my mother, who is a nurse in a dermatologist office, and explained to her what happened. She looked at my foot, and it turned out the glass splintered off into tiny pieces deep into my foot, and now it had to be cut and dug out. Long story short, it took her and another doctor to get it all out. They shot needles into the area to numb me and proceeded to dig until all the shards were out. As you can imagine, it was excruciating pain that could have been avoided if I dealt with it rather than pushed it aside. If I would have just addressed it when it first occurred and pulled it out, then tiny pieces of glass would not have broken off and tried to infect the rest of my foot.

Exposing pain hurts. Cleaning out wounds can take a lot of courage. And, yes, trying to heal a hurt might slow you down. But an infection can cause extreme damage over time.

When we get numbed, it does not mean we are healed. When doctors numb you, that is not the part that heals you. It simply masks the pain that is going on deeper beneath the surface. They numb you so they can get to where the real problem is. Do not mistake numbness for healing. We have to expose the wound and let God clean it out. You must take the time to address areas of hurt so they do not infect areas around them.

At the time I was dealing with this toxic relationship between Jacob and me, I was also leading an intimate prayer group. God was calling me to be open to them, to be vulnerable. I had to surrender. It was in that prayer room true healing began. I opened my mouth and was transparent. I admitted what I was going through and didn't allow the shame to have a place anymore. I exposed the hate in my heart. And when I confronted the problem, I got to the root of it. I was waiting for a sorry. A sorry that would never come. A sorry that wouldn't change the damage already done. I was waiting to forgive only when he apologized, only when he deserved it. But God was calling me to forgive now, calling me to expose the hurt in my heart, because the part of your heart you don't let God into becomes a playground for the enemy.

Numbness simply masks the pain that is going on deeper beneath the surface.

I broke down. I did not even recognize the sobs coming out of my mouth as I was surrounded by my close prayer family. They all embraced me, put hands on me, and prayed over me. They just let me break.

I let go. It felt supernatural, like Jesus was embracing me with His loving arms, holding me, telling me it was going to be okay, that I did not have to fake it. I did not have to wear my "leader" face. In that prayer moment, I let God remove the walls I did not even realize were there. As I released control, I released my tears, and He took my shame. He took my hate. He took my bitterness. He even took my brokenness.

This could not happen until I opened my mouth and admitted that I needed God's help, that alone I could not fix this. No time or avoidance was going to do it either. God's words had to be in that area of my heart. I had to rip out the painful, toxic ones. I was not even aware that the damage went so deep in my heart.

Scripture says many times that God's word needs to be written on our hearts. If we do not have His word written on our hearts, then someone else's is. The Bible is very clear about the power of our thoughts.

When Jacob spoke words of anger, hurt, and lies over me, I let them sit. "You're crazy. Why do you think people actually care what you have to say? You're too passionate. You do not deserve nice things. You care too much." I went over them again and again. I let them cut deep, re-playing them until I believed them. God's words in that area were not on my heart. Instead unworthy was. Not loveable. Too broken. Too messed up. Undeserving of a kind, respectful love. To me, love looked painful, full of cheating, avoidance, lies, and darkness. Stones stacked up lie by lie, and the walls that were never meant to be built grew higher.

God's tender love couldn't reach it until I allowed Him in and let Him uproot what was hidden in my heart. I thought it was just something that could stay numb, tucked away, a time in my life that could be forgotten, something I would have to face alone because it was just too dark. I was ashamed. The walls that were created kept God's words from getting in, and the pain was threatening to infect other areas.

If God's word is not written on our hearts, then someone else's is.

What needs healing in your heart? What do you need to expose and clean out? Whom do you need to forgive right now? What do you need to surrender? Are there words that were spoken to you that you actually started to believe? An old pain that you have let become numb and calloused? Someone that you have put on the list of unforgivable? Someone you cannot even pray for because they hurt you so bad? Someone that has mistreated you one too many times? Someone who walked over you again and again? Something that has caused so much damage to your heart you feel beyond repair? Well, I have some news for you. Jeremiah 23:29 says, "'Is not my word like fire,' declares the LORD, 'and like a hammer that breaks a rock in pieces?'"

It is not too late to change what lies you have written on your heart. The walls you have built stand no match for the word of God no matter how painful, ugly, or hidden they are. The word of God is like a hammer that breaks rocks into pieces.

Name-calling and harsh words echoed in my head for a very long time. Jabbing statements hurt me to the core. But they are no match for what my Heavenly Father says about me. God's words set the lies ablaze. His words broke through the walls and demolished every last one of them. His words put a new song in my mouth. I just had to allow Him in. I had to expose the wound for what it was and allow God's control in every area, not just the easy ones.

The same words He speaks over me He speaks over you. Every time a lie comes up, I declare the truth. Lies must flee in the presence of truth. Let your heart be so full of God that it has no room for the lies of the enemy because a heart that is not led by God's words can be manipulated by Satan's lies. We must be full of God's words.

How do I know what God says about me? We find His words in the Bible.

Do not be confused, because sometimes it will feel as though nothing has changed when you speak truth over yourself. Feelings are liars. Declare the words of God over your life consistently despite your feelings. Just like it took time for my heart to harden, it takes time for it to become softened. Forgiveness does not always happen overnight, but it is a consistent choice. It is a choice that is worth it. Take the time daily to speak God's truth over yourself. Remind yourself.

To be honest with you, I did not want to forgive. Jacob did not deserve it in my eyes. I wanted him to hurt as he hurt me time and time again. I wanted him to pay for my suffering, for hurting my heart so deeply. Why should I forgive someone who was not even sorry, who did not even see how much damage they caused? But this was my pain thinking. This was my pain dictating my thoughts. Unforgiveness was not the answer. I could not let darkness lead to more darkness. I had to fight it with light.

Let your heart be so full of God that it has no room for the lies of the enemy.

"At the end of the day, forgiveness is really not for the other person's benefit at all—it's for our own. Regardless of how illogical it may seem at times, it is through unconditional forgiveness that we surrender the past to the past and enter the present, freeing ourselves to stand in the infinite Light that knows how to heal our deepest and most painful wounds," says author Dennis Merritt Jones.[1]

If I could not forgive, then I could not be set free. I could not move forward. To forgive is to let go of the past. Forgiveness is not saying what they did was okay. Forgiveness is not trusting them, it is giving them grace. It is releasing them to God. It is releasing them from a debt they could never repay you. You can never be repaid

---

1 Dennis Merritt Jones, *Your Redefining Moments: Becoming Who You Were Born to Be*, (New York: Tarcher, 2015),12.

for the tears, the heartbreaks, the sleepless nights, the stress. No one can reverse what has been done to you. They cannot erase the scars that they have created. But you can give them to God. God makes scars work beautifully into your story. Let what happened to you build you up, not become your prison. Let God use it for good.

The Bible tells us many times to forgive each other as the Lord forgives us (Eph. 4:32). Who am I to not forgive because the pain was great? God forgives me for all the pain I have caused Him, all the times I have sinned against Him, all the times I have missed Him trying to get my attention or even the times I ran away from Him. He blots them out of His book, remembering them no more.

Forgiveness is not easy, but Jesus says He will give you strength in areas of weakness. The truth is that Jacob was hurting too. Hurt people hurt people. Even while I was writing about this chapter in my life, I had to choose forgiveness again. When my memories have flashed back from time to time, I have had to stop and pray for forgiveness again. Matthew 18:21–22 says, "Then Peter came to Jesus and asked, 'Lord, how many times shall I forgive my brother or sister who sins against me? Up to seven times?' Jesus answered, 'I tell you, not seven times, but seventy-seven times.'" It is a consistent choice, but it is a choice worth making. Having unforgiveness in your heart is too much of a burden to carry, so we must choose forgiveness each time thoughts come back. I promise it does get easier and the sting does go away. Be patient with yourself. Just be consistent.

We should also understand that we are not at war with people. Yes, they might be the tool that is causing pain, but it is the spirit that is behind it. Ephesians 6:12 says, "For we wrestle not against flesh and blood, but against principalities, against powers, against the rulers of the darkness of this world, against spiritual wickedness in high places." Our fight is not with the people but what is at work that we cannot see. We must pray against that darkness. Jesus has given us authority. He has already defeated darkness. This helps with the forgiveness part a little more.

Holding on to bitterness ends up backfiring and keeps you from experiencing love and joy. Do not look at forgiveness as this weak act. Forgiveness is a sign of strength. It is saying that you are strong enough to choose forgiveness despite your feelings. You are strong enough to make a choice to not let past offenses keep you from future peace.

Think of the people you need to forgive and what you need to surrender. I know it hurts. The pain that they have caused may have been great. You might be losing sleep over it or even hurting other relationships because of it. Christ has already set you free on the cross. Let joy and love back into your heart. Do not let unforgiveness rob you one minute longer. Do not let unforgiveness hold you captive. Do not let it trap you in offense. It is not your burden to hold on to what has happened to you. Let it go—they could never repay you. But God can step in the gap.

Let us be open in this moment of prayer. If you have to cry, cry. If you have to scream, scream. If you have to break, break. Go to Him in spirit and in truth. Be okay with not being okay. Be honest with God. Let Him start removing the bricks one by one.

PRAYER:

Heavenly Father, I need you. Truth is, I have been holding on to this offense, letting it fester. The pain they have caused me is turning me bitter and numb. I do not want to have hate in my heart. But, to be honest, it hurts to even pray for them. So I know that I cannot do this without you. I come before your throne and remind you of your word. You say that your word is like a hammer. I give you the authority to break down every wall, every offense, every calloused area in my heart. I need you to soften and speak to those areas. I want to forgive them as you have forgiven me. Please help me do this. I surrender this over to you, as you say you carry my burdens. Thank you, Lord, for your help. Thank you that I never have to do these difficult things alone, that I can always count on you. Thank you for hearing the cries of my heart. I pray you grow my heart, grow its capacity to trust you. Thank you for never leaving my side. I love you. In Jesus's name, amen.

CHAPTER 7

WILD AND ALONE

If you could be any animal, what would you be? An elephant, a bird, a tiger?

I would be a jaguar. Not only are they stunning creatures, but they fascinate me. They can exist on land, in water, or up in the trees, beautiful and vicious all at the same time. I love the way they throw their weight around as they run fearlessly through the trees or how they swim with elegance. Their name comes from the word *yaguar,* which means "he who kills in one leap." That name alone is pretty impressive. They will eat almost anything, even a thick-skinned crocodile. The only predator they have in the wild is humans. My favorite trait is its speed, the way it runs so effortlessly.

Although I was never quite as fast or as elegant, running was one of my escapes. I have used it as a method of release since middle school. There is something about it for me. Running made me feel in control, because things often felt so out of control. I could push as hard as I wanted, go for however long my body would take, exert myself until my lungs gasped for breath. I got to decide when enough was enough. It felt like an escape.

My brain is always on overdrive, always processing, always thinking, constantly going a mile a minute. But when I would run, I would be forced to focus on my breath if I wanted to get far. Focus until the thoughts swirling around my head were pounding under my feet. I would run as if I could run away from everything. Problems. Boys. Myself. The past or even the future.

One evening I needed to go for a run. I was desperate to get away, desperate to gain control; my thoughts were spiraling again. I could not get out of this relationship circle with Jacob that was desperately trying to break my heart. That was determined to be front and center in my mind. No matter if we were "dating" or not, my heart always seemed to wander back to him. It had been six years on and off, for crying out loud. Things between us seemed beyond complicated, each one of us too afraid to fully commit, too hurt from the past to want to let our guards down. *When will this end? Can I ever get over him? Will this dull pain ever go away? How long will this hurt? What am I missing? Why does this keep happening?*

Knowing it was going to rain, I decided to run barefoot, which I did often, as I lived by the beach. I loved the feel of the ground beneath my feet. I could smell the rain break through the air, see it in the way the trees swayed in the wind. As I started out in my routine jog through the thick forest trail, the damp, warm ground felt good on my feet. The wind was loud and cool on my face. There was so much on my mind. I could literally feel the weight of my thoughts. So many choices to make. Too many. They seemed to weigh as much as the trees I jogged past.

The weight seemed to make my steps twice as heavy. It was like my thoughts wanted to crush me, keep me from moving forward, not let me escape. I picked up my speed. Run.

The weight that started in my mind made its way down. My lungs felt heavy; each breath grew tighter. I didn't even notice the rain that started as a drizzle and was now a downpour. I was thinking myself into a panic. *What am I supposed to do? How can I make these choices? God, please help me. I am losing it again.*

My pace was now just under a sprint. The thoughts had all my attention, not my pounding heart. *Lord, I cannot do this. Wasted time, wasted tears. I thought it was the real thing, how could I be so wrong? I am not equipped for this. I cannot be who you have called me to be. This seems just too much. You promised You are with me, so where are You?*

Faster I ran, trying to escape my reality, fleeing from decisions that awaited me back at my apartment. *God, I do not want to do this anymore. I am losing this fight.* My breath was rigid; my lungs now felt like they were taking the full weight of my thoughts. Barefoot, sprinting through the trail, rain pouring out like it was quenching a fire, I am sure I looked like a wild child out in the wilderness. I looked as if I were running like my life depended on it. It sure felt like it. If I stopped, I knew it would all catch up with me and the tears would start to flow. *Run.*

Stuck in my own head, I was surrounded by the wilderness. My lungs wanted to give way, as did my legs.

Now in full sprint, arms pumping by my sides, I sought one thing: escape. *Why, God? Why did you save me? Why did you call me for this? Take this pain away. I do not want to love anymore. I don't even want to hope for love anymore, it always ends in pain. I just can't do this.*

I did not see the flooded path coming up around the bend. Over my thoughts, over my pain, over my body that was warning me this speed was not sustainable, I felt God loud and clear.

"You are right, you cannot do this on your own. So let me help you."

When I rounded the bend, my overexerted body was welcomed by the flood of puddles. I lost my footing; down I went, hard, sliding on the path toward the bushes, not even attempting to catch my fall.

"Stop running and let go."

Pain shot up through my right hip and leg that took the brunt of the slide. It was nothing but a dull throb compared to the pain of my insides, the pain of giving in, the pain of breaking, the pain of letting go. I stopped trying to have control and let it all go. I gave in to God and allowed Him to break the walls once again, the ones I placed brick by brick, hoping they would mask my mess. I let go of my what-ifs. Let go of my desire to make this relationship last. Let go of all the love that I put in the wrong place.

There on the ground, I was confronted with a hard task. God was telling me to let go, to walk away from the six-year relationship, something I poured a lot into, sacrificed for, lost sleep over. I cried to God, telling Him that He knew how much this hurt. God knew how much I loved this man. God simply reminded me that He loves me more. That was the truth I needed to remind myself of: God's love is enough.

God loves you more than you could ever love anyone. He has a love that fights for you. A love that is jealous for you. A love that chases after you. A love that makes fear and darkness run away. A love that never fails, never lets you down, never forgets about you.

If my hope and value were in a man, or any other person for that matter, I would keep ending up here in the wilderness. I would keep running. I would keep losing. I would continue to wind up empty, unsatisfied, hurt. People or things cannot fill God-sized holes. I let the tears flow down right into the mess I was still sitting in.

In the wilderness, I broke down. He was right. I had to let go. I had to stop trying to do it on my own, stop running, stop putting on a face. I needed His help. Breaking had to occur so growth could begin. I had to stop putting my hope in a man and begin putting it in God. You can't overcome what you don't confront. And I needed to put God on the throne instead of this relationship. I was smack-dab in the middle of my wilderness season.

Each person growing in Christ goes through their own wilderness season, a season of isolation. How do I know this? Because the Bible shows us this. Jesus was in the wilderness for forty days and forty nights. Moses fled to the wilderness after he committed murder. The great prophet Elijah went on a day's journey that turned into forty days and nights of the wilderness. The Israelites were in the wilderness for forty years! Jonah spent three days in the belly of a fish, dark and alone. David was alone in the field tending to a flock. Gideon hid in the winepress.

People or things cannot fill God-sized holes.

Let's take a look at Moses in Exodus. Moses was abandoned as a child and raised in a palace, an outsider to his own people and not fitting in with the ones who raised him. He committed murder, then he ran. Moses made a home out in the wilderness season. It was right there in the comfort of his wilderness that God showed up, just like He met me in mine. There is no outrunning God.

How do you know you're in a wilderness? First off, you can't miss it. Let's look at the definition.[2]

1. Uncultivated - It has no use for growing crops.

2. Uninhabited - No one else lives there, no man or animals.

3. Inhospitable - Harsh and difficult environment to live in.

---

2 "Wilderness: Definition of Wilderness by Oxford Dictionary on Lexico.com," Lexico Dictionaries | English (Lexico Dictionaries, 2020), https://www.lexico.com/en/definition/wilderness.

Uncultivated
Are you in a season where nothing seems to be growing? You are trying, but your efforts seem to be useless. Trying to work the land. Trying to grow the relationship, the business, the family, the ministry. But everything just keeps dying. No matter what you plant, the weeds just choke it out. That is the wilderness.

Uninhabited
Are you in a season where no one else is there? You feel alone, forgotten, abandoned, where it seems no one understands what you are going through or you couldn't tell them even if you tried. You could even find yourself alone in a room full of people. That is the wilderness.

Inhospitable
Are you in a season that is difficult? That is so harsh that just to survive you must give it everything you got? You have to fight every day to get up. Fight for your peace of mind. Fight for your joy. Fight against fear. Surrounded by opposition and trials. That is the wilderness.

We can often compartmentalize the wilderness. We can section it off. We can make it secret, where we can still walk around and do our daily routines, but in our heads, we are miles away, present but gone, in the conversations but not listening. It can be sectioned to our job situation, our joy, our relationships, our purpose, or our calling. There is that one thing, that one area, that seems to not grow. It can be a silent struggle, something you are alone in.

I don't know how long you have been in that place, but I do know that it can seem like you are forgotten. Maybe this one season seems to be a lot longer than you anticipated. You might think you just have to deal with it, make your home there like Moses. The wilderness can seem to be full of wandering. There are no paths either, no paved roads, no stoplights, no directions. This is a place of uncertainty with nothing to show you where to go. But this is also a place of just you and God.

I want you to know that God is in the wilderness. Even in this dead wasteland, He is in control. He is fighting for you, and He is still directing you. It may seem like you have been walking around in it for days, months, or even years, but His timing is perfect. He comes down to this place and speaks to you right in the middle of it. In this deserted place that seems lonely, He is forming you, building you, pruning you. He sees you there just like He saw Moses. Exodus 3:2 says, "There the Angel of the Lord showed Himself to Moses in a burning fire from inside a bush." He shows up in this place of uncertainty, this place of desolation. You cannot run away from the love of God. It chases you down. It will follow you right out into your wilderness.

Just like David, who had to kill the bear and the lion in his wilderness before he would conquer Goliath, Moses had to learn who he was in his wilderness before leading the people of Egypt. Jesus was tempted by Satan every step of the way in His wilderness. Your wilderness is not meant to be a permanent place but a place that prepares you for the next. A place you pass through. A place that God is working with you and on you one on one.

To be honest, when I look back, I can say that I am thankful that He worked some things out in the wilderness. I am very grateful He helped me get rid of some things in private so I could be prepared when I went out in public. The isolation was crushing, but it was where I truly learned dependence on God. I learned to stop running and start facing the work that needed to take place in my heart, to stop hiding it and start letting it go. God is and will always be enough for me—I just had to see it. He was the fullness I was so desperately seeking. No man, no job, no different state could give me what I was on the run for: the fullness of God.

Your wilderness is not meant to be a permanent place but a place to prepare you for the next season.

This truth is powerful. God is enough, and He is in you.

I am still on the road to rewiring my thoughts on the matter. I did not learn the easy way. I was ready to put up a fight in my wilderness. I was going to find what I was missing. I had a great job, a degree in finance, and was starting to really find my place in the church. I guess you can say I looked good on paper.

But God doesn't look at what we look at—He looks at our hearts. That was where I was a mess. I still did not have Him completely on the throne of my life. I was seeking value and affirmation in a relationship that was not centered around God. My hope was not rested in Him, it was in my works and my relationships. I did not understand this at once; it took time. It was not until I lost it all, until I was left in shambles on the floor, until I was heartbroken again and again. Only when it seemed I had nothing did I see where my hope really was put.

I could sing of my love for God on the beautiful mountaintop, but what about in the dry, desolate wilderness? I was so grateful when my life was going great and according to my plan, but what about when it didn't? This is the second wilderness I want to talk about because I have been in quite a few different wilderness seasons. One was like Moses where I ran to flee from my past. One was like David in secret training. But I want to talk about the one of Elijah, the one where you go to give up, the not-so-glamorous wilderness. This is the one that tries to consume you, the one that seems to be too much for you.

Elijah was afraid and ran for his life. When he came to Beersheba in Judah, he left his servant there, while he himself went a day's journey into the wilderness. He came to a broom bush, sat down under it and prayed that he might die. "I have had enough, LORD," he said. "Take my life; I am no better than my ancestors." Then he lay down under the bush and fell asleep.

All at once an angel touched him and said, "Get up and eat." He looked around, and there by his head was some bread baked over hot coals, and a jar of water. He ate and drank and then lay down again.

The angel of the Lord came back a second time and touched him and said, "Get up and eat, for the journey is too much for you." So he got up and ate and drank. Strengthened by that food, he traveled forty days and forty nights until he reached Horeb, the mountain of God. There he went into a cave and spent the night.

The Lord said, "Go out and stand on the mountain in the presence of the Lord, for the Lord is about to pass by."
—1 Kings 19:3–7, 11

This is the great prophet Elijah who, in 1 Kings 18, prayed fire down from the sky and killed 850 false prophets! And yet within the next few days he lay down to give up his life, full of so much fear that he could not take another step. This story speaks to me so much because, as you have read, I have been there myself. I lay myself down to die, gave up. I could not see past the day that was trying to drown me. I know how it feels.

The truth is even in this time God shows up. He is so faithful to you, full of grace and mercy. Just like He sent the angel there to provide for Elijah, He can provide for you.

There are a few takeaways from this scripture that have helped me get up no matter how many times I was found on my face.

- After our greatest victory, great discouragement can often follow.

Every mountain we climb has an uphill, a peak, and a downside. Life is full of ups and downs. We get a choice. We get to decide what we are anchored on. If your anchor is feelings, you will always be getting tossed around. The enemy does not want you walking around in victory. He comes immediately to steal your faith (Matt. 13:4). We must be anchored in God, rooted in His word so that when the lies come, we can see them for what they are: lies. We must write God's word on our hearts so that when fear comes, it stands no chance—we are already anchored (Prov. 7:3). If Scripture clearly tells us the enemy comes immediately to steal our faith, then we should not be caught off guard when he tries; instead, we can be ready.

- Isolation is a dangerous place to be.

Elijah isolated himself, sent away the one person (his servant) that was meant to help him. We tend to do this a lot. When we are hurting or being crushed, we flee. We stop going to church, stop reading the word, stop hanging out with our closest friends. When we are overwhelmed with sorrow and feelings of defeat, we tend to isolate. We don't want anyone around.

You can silence your phone, lock the world out, cut everyone off. I have been there way too many times. The pain, the letdown, the hurt, they can immobilize you from life.

This is an unsafe spot to be.

I cannot stress this enough: isolation makes you more susceptible to the thoughts that are not accurate! The enemy wants you in this place, alone in your head, alone in your feelings, alone with your stress, your pain, your anxiety. He wants to get you from victory to lying down to die. The enemy wants you to think that you are all alone and that no one can possibly understand the hurt or pain that you are feeling. He wants you to think that no one gets the betrayal you feel, wants you to think that you're not valued or loved enough for anyone to even care.

These are all lies!

There in the forest on the floor, I was alone in my lies. I was mad, thinking, *God, you saved my life for this, to be taken out by a heartbreak!* My mind went back to my suicide attempt ten years ago. When I got home from the hospital, I knew I had some serious problems when I realized I wasn't even concerned that I was moments away from losing my life and instead was more focused on the shame of failing everyone. I had been carrying this weight around silently on my back, this weight of depression and of no self-worth, and I was now exposed to the whole world, to my family, to my friends. I could no longer hide it; I could no longer pretend that everything was fine, that I was okay. My thinking was so defective, and now everyone knew it!

I felt so alone in my failure and in my shame, but that was a lie. I was surrounded by a concerned family and loving friends. I was surrounded by God. I was not a failure. It was not a weakness—it was a sickness. I was sick with depression, sick with the wrong image of myself. I would lock myself in the bathroom, run the shower, and break down, shutting out my family, shutting out the mess I made, sitting in my guilt. I was ignoring the truth that I needed help, that everything was not okay. I needed a support system. I needed to be open and transparent with those around me. I needed God.

I felt like Elijah out in the wilderness. I had lain down and begged God to take this from me. *Take this from me, I can't do it anymore! Why did you save me?* I was disconnecting myself, leaving all the people back in Beersheba, alone and detached. This was right where the enemy wanted me. If God did not let my life slip away back when I swallowed pill after pill, then He sure was not going to let this relationship take me out.

But he led his own people like a flock of sheep, guiding them safely through the wilderness. He kept them safe so they were not afraid; but the sea covered their enemies.
—Psalm 78:52–53 (NLT)

Even in the wilderness, God has planned the place. God showed up. He already had a story written. He already had a provision in place. All I had to do was get up. God had already sent angels to meet Elijah, to touch him and give him sustenance.

Just get up. God will always call you out of brokenness. It is your choice to get up or stay down in the affliction.

Even when we want to give up, our great God will never give up on us. He knows the journey you are about to take in this wilderness is going to be too much for you. The journey of healing. The journey of seeing your worth. The journey of dependence on God. But He has already made the provisions.

God never left you in the wilderness, just like He did not leave me to die there in my room. He sent provision that touched me and said, "Open your eyes, for this fight is too much for you. Just get up and drink some water, eat some bread." He knew the journey ahead was going to be hard, but He sustained me. God never leaves us in this place alone. He is there guiding us to safety.

God will always call you out of brokenness. It is your choice to get up or stay down in the affliction.

I don't know what you are silently struggling with, but I do know God sees you. He is Emmanuel, God with us. I do know that He wants to use your wilderness. Scripture says in Romans 8:28 that He uses *all* things for good. He knows that sometimes it's hard to think straight and those feelings can seem crushing and overwhelming. They can blur your vision. But once we have accepted Christ as our Savior, we can have an eternal mind-set. We can have an eternal perspective. This is a mere moment in time, and God will use this for good. And, yes, it might be easier to say you're okay and everything is fine. But He has called you not for easy but for greatness. He has a purpose for your life that only you can fulfill. You have something in you that the world needs. God wants to use you! Do not let this season of wilderness immobilize you. Just keep getting up. Let Him sustain you!

A few years after my attempt at suicide, I was walking into my class at university. And who would have known I would answer a phone call from my sister telling me that she just couldn't take it, that the struggle was too much for her. Her life was falling apart, and she just didn't have the fight in her anymore. She lived far away and was silently struggling. Her fiancé at the time was dealing with addiction, and she could not bear it. She wanted to end her life. She was all the way in New York, isolated in her wilderness.

God knew this was going to happen, that as I battled my wilderness, my sickness, I was in training to coach someone through it down the road. And in the moment, I could just listen to her. I could be there for her. I could tell her she was not alone. I could remind her that this is only temporary. She could not make a permanent decision on a temporary pain. Her life is so much more than this mere moment. I could speak life to her because God showed me the value in mine. I could speak love and compassion because God showed it to me in my wilderness. Now, years later, my sister just had her first baby and is beyond happy. Praise God!

God will use every single ounce of your pain—just get up! None of your wilderness will go to waste. Just like Moses shepherding the people. Just like Elijah, who got to experience the presence of the Lord on that mountain. Just like me getting to minister to suicidal people down the road. I know it's hard, but He has provisions on the way. Get up and tell those lies the truth. Tell those feelings that they can't remain; take them captive.

Yes, I am overwhelmed, but my God fights for me.

Yes, I feel despair, but my God is close to the brokenhearted.

Yes, I cannot see the way out, but my God can part seas and move mountains for me.

- Choose to get up despite everything that is telling you to stay down.

Choose to not listen to the lies one minute longer. You are victorious. You are a mighty warrior. You are enough. You are chosen. You are cared for by the King of all Kings. You are called His friend, child, and masterpiece. It is okay if you do it afraid. It is okay to do it unsure. Just get up!

Many times this is all we can manage to do, just like Elijah. We have been broken so badly, betrayed deeply by someone close too many times, let down by someone we gave our all to, left by those we thought we could count on, or struggled for so long that we have come to the end of the rope. All we can do is get up. Get up, eat some crappy food, then go back to bed. Get up, eat a gallon of ice cream, and blankly stare at a TV screen. Get up, look at your responsibilities, and then shut the door on them. Get up, go to counseling, and don't say a word. God wanted Elijah to just *get up*. He would do the rest. God will fight for you—just show up.

After remembering that wilderness that I had lain down to die in that God had already brought me through, I got up from my puddle. Walked back to my place. Cleaned off the dirt and blood from my fall. Had the hard conversation with Jacob and let my relationship go. Prayed for God to break the chains and strongholds attached, and we shut the door on our past together.

Simple, but not easy. Crushing, but it did not kill me. Painful, but full of purpose. If God was faithful back then in my darkest days, then He would be now. I put my trust in Him; there was no more plan B. I let go and grabbed ahold of God.

The peace that I experienced after that crushing moment was far beyond anything I had ever experienced before. It did not mean I did not have thoughts of my past or that I did not miss the relationship. It did mean that each time I did, I would thank God for His faithfulness. I would thank God for the plans He has for me in the future. I would thank Him that His presence is enough for me. I reminded my spirit to let go and grab God each time.

Take a moment of true transparent reflection. Confront the wall you need to break down or the thing you need to let go of. Or maybe you need to take something out of the place where God wants to be. Look at the wilderness you are in and see what God is doing in it. You will pass through this! Nothing is without purpose. It will prepare you for the next place. Just get up, and know if He is for you, what can stand against you?

God loves you too much to let you do this on your own. You might not be able to carry it, but He can. You might not be able to heal it, but He can. You might not understand it, but He does. Just keep getting up and lean on Him. His word does not fail. Look at these scriptures below before you go into a moment of prayer. Remind your spirit what God said concerning you.

- Psalm 46:10: "He says, 'Be still, and know that I am God; I will be exalted among the nations, I will be exalted in the earth.'"

- Deuteronomy 20:4: "For the LORD your God is the one who goes with you to fight for you against your enemies to give you the victory."

- Isaiah 54:17 (ESV): "No weapon that is fashioned against you shall succeed, and you shall confute every tongue that rises against you in judgment. This is the heritage of the servants of the LORD and their vindication from me, declares the LORD."

- Psalm 34:17 (ESV): "When the righteous cry for help, the LORD hears and delivers them out of all their troubles."

- Isaiah 41:10 (ESV): "Fear not, for I am with you; be not dismayed, for I am your God; I will strengthen you, I will help you, I will uphold you with my righteous right hand."

- Isaiah 43:2 (ESV): "When you pass through the waters, I will be with you; and through the rivers, they shall not overwhelm you; when you walk through fire you shall not be burned, and the flame shall not consume you."

PRAYER:

Lord, I need you. This place of desolation is overwhelming. No matter how much I try to run, my troubles outnumber me. This fight, this battle, they are too much to take. I am tired of it being so hard. You say do not be dismayed. You say you will strengthen me. That the waters, rivers, fire, flames, none of them will consume me. That you hear me and will deliver me from *all* my troubles. I speak your words over my wilderness. I speak truth over these intense feelings. Anchor me on your word. I do not want to be tossed to and fro anymore. I cast this to you and trust that it is in your hands. I trust you in every area of my life. Help me to see what you are teaching me in this season. Remove anything that I might have put in front of you. May your love cast out this fear and anxiety. In Jesus's name, amen.

CHAPTER 8

LET'S TALK ABOUT IT

Surprised by Steven's late-night phone calls, I silenced the phone and rolled back to bed. If he really needed something, he would leave a voicemail, and that he did.

"Heather, call me, I need to talk," he said in a strange but calm voice.

Through the years, he and I grew apart but always were there for each other. We wrote letters to one another when I was away in college and kept in contact when I moved back home. Our love never went beyond our friendship, and we both were okay with that, although I did tease him a lot for breaking my heart in middle school. We had a lot to tease each other for from the sixth grade to my first year in college.

For a lot of our relationship, Steven was getting in and out of trouble, and that never seemed to go away. He went to jail a few times—I do not recall why—but one sentence was for way too long. I would eagerly await his letters, and sometimes I would even get to visit him with his mom. He would also get time to call me, which were highlights of my day. He was so easy to talk to, and he just understood me. When he finally got out, he swore it was going to be his last time, and he really seemed to be turning the page for the better. Months went by, and we lost some contact, but he seemed fine. I was on my bed when I got the call.

It seems that time stands still in traumatic moments. That even if days, months, or years pass by, you can always go back to the exact moment certain pain was afflicted. Some people can pinpoint music playing or smells in the environment the day they were left behind. Some can remember the exact day someone put their hands on them, the day they snapped, the day they were told they were no longer loved. Many can recall the day someone they loved passed away, the day they reached the end of their rope, the day they couldn't face life. Some remember the moment the crash happened that changed everything.

I can remember them all as if time stood still, as if the earth stopped moving on its axis. They are painful memories that have been etched into my thoughts playing their own little movie. I can recall how the air seemed to get rigid and suffocating. I can remember how my breath took so much effort to move in and out of my lungs. I can remember the swirling feeling of my thoughts rapidly spinning in my head.

I can remember thinking, *How will I ever get past this?* The moments that do not seem like moments and are rather stretched-out pauses of time. The moments that seem to punch you hard in the gut, daring you to get up. I can recall holding my chest, feeling if I released the pressure I would shatter into tiny pieces on the floor like that little broken vase. The moments that seem to change things in the largest or even the slightest way. I often wonder if these memories will fade.

I remember the very place I was sitting when Steven's mom called me to tell me he took his life. The sentence left this void in the air. It dangled there until the silence from the other line became deafening to my ears. The room halted as my mind spun. The blaring TV became silent. *Come on, brain, say something. Anything. Respond.*

Gone. He was gone. What do I say to that? No words seemed like the right choice. No sentence could articulate the loss. I wanted to ask if she was sure. I wanted this to be a sick prank. *What if I answered? What if I could have stopped him? What if...*The "what-ifs" became the monster in the room.

In the back row of the funeral, I could not utter a word. My eyes stayed zoomed in on the floor like it held the secrets of the world. Like it had the answers to the questions that I could not seem to find. I think I replayed his voice message over a thousand times, just holding on to what I had left.

I met with his mother over the course of several weeks after. We would talk and continue to check on each other. It strangely made me feel closer to him being there with her, although it was hard to look into her eyes. They were so full of pain; sorrow was spilling out of them. I wanted to make her stop crying, but how? I wanted to hug her tight. I wanted to remove all the pain she felt, tell her that it was all going to be okay, that she was strong, just like we would console each other when we would visit him in jail. I wanted to convince her that she could get through this too. Like somehow I knew, but I had no idea. How could I console a grieving mother?

I remember begging God to give me her pain, pleading with Him to transfer it to me. I could take it for her; I knew I could handle it. Pain seemed to always have a way of finding me, even when self-inflicted. I felt twenty going on fifty. I have seen death look me in the eyes. I have seen death take others away and it threaten those around me. The darkness of depression seemed to loom around and hang out with death, the two going everywhere together.

I snapped back into the room; it has been six years since Steven has passed away. "Are you uncomfortable sharing your stories?" my friend Jane asked.

I had just finished preaching a Sunday service at church. I felt her heavy heart from across the room. "Not anymore," I replied, remembering the first time how scared I was to be open about my struggles. I could feel her getting ready to ask another question with hesitation.

"How long have you wrestled with it?" she continued softly while staring down at the floor.

My heart jumped for joy. I knew where this was going, as this had happened almost every time I had shared a testimony about suicide in a public setting.

"How do you deal with your depression now?" she asked. "I am not so good at dealing with mine or even talking about it. People really do not even know I struggle with it."

And just like that, the door opened for me to minister into Jane's life, to speak God's love and compassion over her.

Your story is important. You have no idea who is listening, looking, clinging on to hope. I have seen it time and time again. I share my story as if little girls like me were planning their last days or troubled kids like Steven were losing the battle and getting ready to pull the trigger. I share my story for the people who think they are crazy with their constant emotional ups and downs. For the people that are giving in to the lies of the enemy that think they just have to deal with what was handed to them. For the people that let shame and guilt drag their head down the path of unworthiness. For the people that want to share but are afraid of being judged. For the people that are so down in their darkness that they cannot see light anymore. For the people that are looking for a glimpse of hope. For the people that have lost their fight. I share because we do not really know what is going on the other side of that so-perfect smile other people wear.

You are light for the world. A city cannot be hidden when it is located on a hill. No one lights a lamp and puts it under a basket. Instead, everyone who lights a lamp puts it on a lamp stand. Then its light shines on everyone in the house. In the same way let your light shine in front of people. Then they will see the good that you do and praise your Father in heaven.

—Matthew 5:14–16 (GW)

You are a light. The enemy does not care if you go to church. He does not even care if you read the Bible. He knows the scriptures; he twisted them around, trying to tempt Jesus in the desert. What he is afraid of is when you act on the scriptures and when you are fully convinced of the goodness of God. I think it sends him trembling when you know who you are in Christ Jesus and the power that is in you because He is in you.

I believe whatever is constantly under attack in your life is what you really need to be paying attention to. Since I was a little girl, the enemy has been attacking my voice, trying to shut me up, using people closest to me to do it. People that I love and look up to tore into my self-esteem, telling me no one cared about what I had to say, telling me I should not talk about my struggle with depression. That I should keep my head down to get by. That I was too passionate. Too involved in church. Too different. It went from me being the too-depressed girl to me being the girl that smiles too much. It began to annoy people that I was too joyful.

I allowed the guilt and shame of my issues to keep me captive for a long time—until I discovered it could be my weapon, until I realized Jesus held all the answers in His word. When my mind stood on God's word, Satan's lies were useless.

I came to understand that each one of my scars was there for a purpose. Every single battle was a chance to show people how God showed up and showed off in my life. Every single scar was a reminder that God is faithful in *every* season.

But Jesus said, "No, go home to your family, and tell them everything the LORD has done for you and how merciful he has been."
—Mark 5:19

I will praise you to all my brothers; I will stand up before the congregation and testify of the wonderful things you have done.
—Psalm 22:22

Come and listen, all you who fear God, and I will tell you what he did for me.
—Psalm 66:16

I cannot help but share because He took me from the pit time and time again and set my feet on solid rock. That, my friend, is what He wants to do for you. He wants to use your story, your scars. So let's talk about it. What is the enemy shaming you with right now? What do you think disqualifies you from God's grace, love, and mercy?

I cannot tell you how many people are suffering right now because they think they are too broken for God to use. How many people I have asked to come with me to church that think they are not wanted there because they are full of sin. Let us take a stand right now! Do not let the enemy shame you for your struggle. I promise there is someone in your community dealing with something similar. God will get the glory. He will turn it around! People will be able to look back over your life and say, "Only God could have done that."

At the beginning of my walk with Jesus, it was a process. I had moments that I was not proud of. There were times I showed up on Sunday still intoxicated from the night before. Times where I was so angry at God for the pain I felt. Times I wanted to walk away from Him yet again. Times when I did not know how to trust God. Times I thought it was His voice, but it was really mine I was following. Times I was volunteering and still depressed. I did not know who to talk to because it seemed like everyone at church was all "blessed and highly favored." What was wrong with me? Why was this Christian walk so hard? Was I the only one falling left and right? I felt if I told the truth I would be judged and, worse, disqualified. I was confused. Was anyone else on this struggle bus with me, or was I the only rider? And if I opened up, would I get thrown out?

I am telling you this because that is not true. I had to stop putting up a front and start building on the word of God if I really wanted transformation. There was no point in pretending I was not struggling. You cannot build something real off something that is fake. When I opened my heart up and surrendered this need to hide my issues, that was when the weight was lifted. When I stopped putting on a front and allowed others to see my not-so-pretty parts, that was when I could get advice and true help. Do not let shame keep you from coming to Jesus. He wants to use it! No matter how "blessed and highly favored" people are, we are all going through something.

So what do we do? What do you do when you're mad at God? When you are depressed? When you are falling apart and it seems like He doesn't care? When your mind is toxic?

Let's take some time to go over some areas we might be lost in, some not-so-popular issues we can experience from time to time, issues that are not talked about often but are still very real. There is freedom in transparency.

First, confront it. What are you actually feeling? Do not brush it off. Do not bury it. Do not discredit it. Face it. There is nothing too big or too small that God does not want to be a part of in your life. He is closer than a brother. He calls Himself your friend. He is the great "I am," Immanuel, God with us, Jehovah Rapha, the Lord that Heals, Jehovah Raah, our shepherd. Nothing can disqualify you or separate you from His perfect love.

I want to confront just a few subjects that we do not hear about too often and give you some tools that have helped me in some areas that, at first, I felt shamed in and was not able to be open about.

Mad at God?

How long, O Lord, will you look on and do nothing? Rescue me from their fierce attacks. Protect my life from these lions! Then I will thank you in front of the great assembly. I will praise you before all the people.

—Psalm 35:17–18

My God, my God, why have you abandoned me? Why are you so far away when I groan for help? Every day I call to you, my God, but you do not answer. Every night I lift my voice, but I find no relief. Yet you are holy, enthroned on the praises of Israel.

—Psalm 22:1–3

Look at David. He was the least of his family. He was a giant slayer. He was chosen to be king. He was a man after God's heart. This man went through a lot of ups and downs, and yet he always cried out to God in honesty. I am not saying we have a right to be going around mad at God. What I am saying is that the reality is sometimes we are. So be honest with God in this place like David was. Tell Him how you really are feeling.

God asks us to come to Him in spirit and in truth. We do not have to hide our feelings from Him or pretend we do not have them. When we are honest, we allow Him into our situation. In James 4, it says we have not because we ask not. Ask God for help! You can even do it mad.

It is okay to feel this way, but do not let this feeling control you. Yes, I might be mad, but I am still going into prayer. Yes, I might not be happy about this, but it will not take my confession away! Give it over to Him.

One of my favorite things about these scriptures is David always chooses to praise God. No matter what, at the end of crying out to God, choose to praise. It is a powerful weapon! Yes, I might be mad at what I am going through, but I choose to still praise Him! Yes, I do not like what is happening, but God is still good, and He is still worthy. We cannot let our attitude or our feelings dictate our praise.

I was mad at God when Steven took his life, confused about why He would let something like that happen. It is hard to see God working something like that out for good. Sometimes it is hard to see good, especially when the suffering becomes personal. But the truth is we have a very personal God who knows what it is like to suffer. Jesus is not indifferent to or distant in your pain or anger. He felt it all when He chose to experience real torment, shed real blood, and die a real death. He did not just suffer like us, He suffered *for* us so that when times come and we cannot bear life's burdens on our own, He can take them for us. He can comfort us. He can have compassion. He can give us strength and peace to overcome. We just have to go to Him.

Remember, your praise might not always match your feelings, but praise Him anyway. You might not want to be thankful, but be thankful anyway. You might not see the good, but declare the goodness of God anyway. There is life and death in our tongue (Prov. 18:21), so choose to speak life out until your environment matches. Hear me when I say this: your environment does not always change, but that does not mean your perspective can't. Choose to praise even if you start off feeling another way.

Ask God for help in prayer and praise Him through it!

Depressed?

The righteous cry out, and the LORD hears them; he delivers them from all their troubles. The LORD is close to the brokenhearted and saves those who are crushed in spirit.
—Psalm 34:17–18

Do not grieve, for the joy of the LORD is your strength.
—Nehemiah 8:10

Be strong and courageous. Do not be afraid or terrified because of them, for the LORD your God goes with you; he will never leave you nor forsake you.
—Deuteronomy 31:6

There are so many verses in the word of God for depression, and yet there are a lot of people battling it daily. Do not feel alone in this. You are not broken or crazy. You do not have to be controlled by your emotions. Scripture says take them captive, arrest them! Trust me, I know how easily emotions can overwhelm you and take control. But Jesus's promise to us is He hears you and is fighting for you.

One of the biggest nuggets of advice I can give you is to talk to someone. Do not wallow in it. Do not let it silently defeat you day by day.

If Jesus is our shepherd, then we are His sheep. Sheep do not go off on their own because then they are vulnerable. When they are alone is when they are picked off by the wolves. Sheep are stronger together and stay in herds for a reason. Isolation is dangerous, especially with depression. So please talk to someone about it! If you do not feel like you have anyone you are comfortable to talk to about it with, then find a Christian counselor and open up to them. Most churches have great resources and will often get you around someone that you can speak with.

Also, if I am feeling depressed, I make sure I am speaking life over myself. Have some verses handy, and speak them over your emotions. Call out the liars, and remind your spirit you have been set free! You are not called to be captive by depression. There are many scriptures that you can turn to and speak out over yourself. Write them down everywhere if you have to.

My battle with depression is not the same as the next person's struggle with it. Your chemical makeup is not the same as mine. What works for me might not work for you. What I am certain of is the power of Jesus, and He is constant. And the word says by His stripes we are healed (Isa. 53:5). I stood in faith and spoke to my mountain of depression to move in Jesus's name (Mark 11:23). I was believing that I was healed of depression, period. That does not mean your faith has to look the same. If you have faith to believe for instant healing, great! If you have the faith to believe with that medication depression will be defeated, that is great too. If you have faith that with counseling and medication you crush depression, bam! Speak to that mountain according to your faith! Either way, God's word is the same, and the outcome is always victory.

Talk to someone, get help! Keep a scriptural confession!

Falling Back into Old Habits?

The godly may trip seven times, but they will get up again.
But one disaster is enough to overthrow the wicked.
—Proverbs 26:16

If we confess our sins, He is faithful and righteous to forgive us our sins and to cleanse us from all unrighteousness.
—1 John 1:9

You are not alone!

This was a hard one for me because the shame came
heavy with it. I thought I could be tougher now that I was
committed to following God. Let's be real, though—just
because I was now saved did not mean that I did not
struggle with temptation. We have to rebuild new habits.

Scripture says if the right hand causes you to sin, cut it
off. I had to stop doing things that I knew I was weak in.
The truth is what you are not changing, you are choosing.
For example, I had to stop going to clubs. I loved to dance,
and I liked to party. But why even tempt myself like that?

Know your weaknesses, and do not tiptoe on them. Do
not even go near the line. Ask God to give you strength,
but also do your part of the work. If you struggle with
porn, why are you watching the most lust-filled films? If
you want to stop partying and getting way too intoxicated,
stop going out with that group of friends to the bar.

Stay strong and ask God for help! Don't just ask Him
for forgiveness after the fact. Call out to Him beforehand
too. Repent and move forward. Do not beat yourself up;
Jesus already paid the price for that. Ask Him to help you

with that specific struggle. Be diligent. Also remember you are not called to perfection but growth. Allow your past to teach you; actually learn from it.

What we continue to focus on we will continue to feed. What we feed will get stronger. What we starve will eventually die. Feed yourself with the word of God and good, pure things. Stop feeding the bad stuff. I had to stop feeding myself negativity and things that were going to make me lust after worldly things. We have to be intentional! The more you deny your flesh, the more you feed your spirit.

God is not taking fun things away from you, He is protecting you from things that cause pain, damage, and loss in the long run. He is protecting you from heartache and afflictions. Ask Him to change and align your desires with His.

Be on guard. Do not tiptoe with temptation. Repent and learn. Be intentional!

Experiencing Grief?
The LORD is close to the brokenhearted and saves those who are crushed in spirit.
—Psalm 34:18
God is our refuge and strength, a very present help in trouble.
—Psalm 46:1
The LORD upholds all who fall and lifts up all who are bowed down.
—Psalm 145:14

Nothing can prepare you for loss. Whether it's sudden or not, grieving is a difficult process. The key word is *process*. It has no time constraints and can come and go in waves as it pleases. As much as our minds try to run, flee, and skip over this overwhelming, crushing emotion of grief, it is part of the healing process. We can try to make sense of what is happening or try to avoid it altogether. Either way, we must embrace grief to move forward.

Jesus knew this feeling all too well. The Bible tells us that even Jesus wept, that even He, the King of Kings, experienced grief. He is close to you, an ever-present help. He uplifts you when you are bowed down. He knows what you are going through and can empathize with you.

Cry out to Him, and allow yourself the time and stillness you need to move over to the healing process. Do not avoid it or push past it. Ask for strength through it. Do not feel the need to rush and where your big-girl or -boy face. Everyone has their own pace and their own method. Find comfort in Scripture, and get still with God. He will make a way through it when there seems no way to recover. He will fill the void that was left behind. Take your time.

Do not rush the process. Get still with God. Let Him fill the void.

I hope you can see a common theme happening here in every single topic. The key is honest prayer, being real, raw, and transparent with yourself and with God. He is big enough to handle your very real emotions. You do not have to share with the whole world; I am not saying post your struggles out there on Facebook. Do open up with some close, faith-filled friends, but most importantly open up with God! Why not let the one who made you, formed you, and loves you help you? My "independent, tough self" learned the hard way. Allow Him in! He does not get offended by us needing to be reassured of His nature. Get in His word, and get it on your heart. Despite the feelings and emotions that you are experiencing, go to Him.

PRAYER:

Lord, I am so grateful that you love me for how I am, emotions and all. I do not have to hide a thing from you—you know my deepest parts. You give me the strength to grow stronger than these emotions. The more I am anchored on you, the less these feelings can toss me around. I come to you with everything I have. I am so grateful there is nothing that can remove me out of your love. Your love that is perfect, that casts out all fear, that never turns its back on me. I surrender over every area in my heart and mind. I need you in it all! Thank you that you are always near. I pray you give me strength in this situation and that you help me to see you in this season. In Jesus's name, amen.

CHAPTER 9

YOU'RE CRAZY

Maybe you have been on the sidelines a lot in your life, watching others around you get prayers answered, experience healing, or have complete transformations. Maybe you've tried your hardest to be cheerful when yet another friend is married or having another kid, and you're over here just trying to keep your head above water. You have been let down and forgotten so many times that just getting by day to day takes enough energy, forget thinking about the future or your "destiny."

On the outside, you have it all together. You even managed to brush your hair and put together an outfit. You look the part, but on the inside, you are screaming for God to show up in your life. He seems to be there for everyone else, but you must have messed up way too many times because He is not responding to you. Maybe you can pray for your friends and family better than you can pray for yourself. Maybe you've always known there was more to life than what you are experiencing daily. You are sick of being on the hamster wheel doing the same circles every day, sick and tired of being run down, doubting your future, and casting your dreams to the side while trying to just get by.

I know I am not the first to tell you, but there really is more. There is more than your mistakes, your pain, your insecurities. Jesus came not just so you can live your life trying to get by. He came for you to live life to the fullest, abundant, fruitful living!

Are you full or drained? Do you have an abundance of joy and peace, or do they seem scarce these days? Are you afraid to move in faith because it seems too uncomfortable and uncertain? I know these feelings all too well.

You can accomplish all that God has for you. What God put in your heart to go after, you have the strength for—it is within you. You are enough because Christ is in you.

Close your eyes for a moment, cast away the thousands of racing thoughts, and focus. Picture that thing you want to change or even that you want to start. Think of the business, the family, the ministry, the music, or the thing you are most passionate about. Think about the generations to come, the legacy you want to leave behind. Think about breaking lack and freeing those down the line from the bondage you have experienced. Think of changing the course of your life as you know it.

Whatever comes to mind right now, you can achieve that. I am not saying it will look the exact way you expect it to, but God put it in your heart for a reason. If God is calling you out into the deep, He will make a way for you there, not to just be "scraping by" but to be living in the fullness of God.

Do not shelve it for another time—the time is now. Your destiny is waiting on you to get up and claim it! People are waiting for you! Industries are waiting on you! God wants to use you, and I am certain of this because you woke up today. There is something in you that the world needs. The time is now to get it out. Today is the time to start writing down the vision, making God-sized goals to move forward to all that God is calling you to.

God wired us all very differently. For some people, like me, the wires can be a little loose and not so organized. For others, their wires are neat and color coordinated on a nice, tidy little shelf. We are all made to walk on our own paths and go down different roads. You are like no one else around you, and neither is your destiny or your story. And thank goodness because that could get really boring. God has a certain race set for you. And I will tell you a secret: you are set up to win!

Therefore, since we are surrounded by such a great cloud of witnesses, let us throw off everything that hinders and the sin that so easily entangles. And let us run with perseverance the race marked out for us, fixing our eyes on Jesus, the pioneer, and perfecter of faith.
—Hebrews 12:1–2

You can get all that God has set before you, which in turn blesses those around you and the generations to come. The impact we can have is surreal when we allow God to work through us. It is so much bigger than we can think or imagine. That is His promise to us. I want us to get our expectations up, want us to fix our gazes up toward God, to the truths that He says about you: "You are a chosen people, a royal priesthood, a holy nation, God's special possession" (1 Pet. 2:9).

Sounds great, right? But how do we do this?

We do it by releasing our faith. "Now faith is confidence in what we hope for and assurance about what we do not see" (Heb. 11:1). Walking in faith is imperative to being all God has called you to be.

Faith's confessions create reality. If it were easy to walk in faith, you would see every Christian walking around in their purpose. We would see a lot more miracles, signs, and wonders here on earth. And let's be honest, we do not. We see a lot of comfy Christians. We see Christians walking around lukewarm and defeated by things that Jesus has already beaten for them.

If this is you right now, please do not beat yourself up. I have been there too. I was confused about why things seemed to be stagnant and unchanging in my life. I had to stop thinking that blessings were only for other people and start believing that they were for me too. I had to stop just talking about faith and start walking it out. It had nothing to do with my prayer life, reading Scripture, or good deeds that I checked off. It had to do with my faith. My belief system. My trust in what God said about me. Me releasing my faith.

So let's look into this faith thing because faith changes everything. It changes the way you talk, the way you lift your head up, the way you walk, everything! I want to simply share some faith seasons I have walked through.

As Scripture says, there is a season for everything under the sun. I believe I have gone through many seasons of faith because faith should be constantly growing, like a muscle. We can start off with tiny faith and grow it to giant-slaying faith. Sometimes faith is rock solid, and sometimes I am not sure where it goes.

For by the grace given me I say to every one of you: Do not think of yourself more highly than you ought, but rather think of yourself with sober judgment, in accordance with the faith God has distributed to each of you.
—Romans 12:3

We each have our own measure of faith. Not all faith looks the same, and this can trip us up because we automatically want that unshakeable faith. Not all faith starts off that way, even for the great faith heroes in the Bible. But I want to encourage you to still believe for the thing, no matter what stage you are in, still have faith even if it feels insignificant, still push toward what God is calling toward you anyway.

Using Scripture, I want to go over different kinds of faith that I think can help us move toward all that God has intended for us. I believe in conditioning our faith. Just like any other discipline, we must grow it and push it past the point of comfort to see results. We cannot be growing our faith and be sitting in comfort. The two do not go hand in hand.

Seed Faith

Having small faith messed me up. I thought this discredited me for a long time. I stopped believing because I thought I was too weak to have that giant-slaying faith like King David. But that is not the truth. Let me prove it to you through Matthew 17:20: "He [Jesus] replied, 'Because you have so little faith. Truly I tell you, if you have faith as small as a mustard seed, you can say to this mountain, "Move from here to there," and it will move. Nothing will be impossible for you.'"

God will use any type of faith you have, even as small as a seed! It is what you do with that seed of faith that matters. Are you speaking it out over the mountains in your way? Are you taking that seed of faith and throwing it out into what God is calling you in? It is not about the size but how we use it, how we exercise it. It is getting that seed faith and throwing it into the hands of God.

Let's not discredit a seed of faith. For some people, a belief as small as a seed takes all the energy that they have. Some people's dreams have been beaten down on for so long that to even have the slightest hope takes all their efforts. Some people have been walked on by every single person they have pitched their idea to and gave up hope. Others gave up on marriage because the last one left a hole so deep, why even hope for better? I see it all the time.

Maybe the enemy has been whispering to you since you were a little kid, planting lies, telling you that you will never amount to anything, you are not bright enough, you will never achieve great things, success is not in your cards, and you are going to end up just like the people you dread. Or maybe your comparisons on Instagram destroyed your seed before it could ever be put into practice. Whatever the case may be, we cannot throw away our seed of faith because even it can move mountains.

I know that sometimes having a seed of faith can seem pointless, and at times, it can be easier to not even put the hope there anymore. To not even hope seems much safer and can't really hurt you, right? No, my friend, I do not think so. You are not getting off that easy. I am asking you to get just a little bit of hope back. There is nothing wrong with just enough faith to get it in God's hands. I can promise you that if you take everything you have got and give it over to God, it changes things. That is when the seed can move mountains. When you throw all the faith you do have into that thing and trust God to fill the gaps, miracles happen. When we come to the end of our strength, that is the perfect setting for God to do what only He can do.

Keep believing even if it seems small, for not all things are what they seem. God is not only a big God but also a still, small voice. He is in the small moments. The scary moments. The doubtful moments. Each is a moment we can trust Him in, even when we cannot trust ourselves. He is faithful in every season. Your faith pleases Him. Take your seed, and run with it. Strong faith is great, but small faith will not be rejected. Ask Him to help you believe again. Keep speaking your faith out loud. Keep declaring the victory of God over that thing.

Jesus said to him, "If you can believe, all things are possible to him who believes." Immediately the father of the child cried out and said with tears, "Lord, I believe; help my unbelief!" Then Jesus healed his child.
—Mark 9:23–25

Cry out to Jesus, and ask Him to help you. Faith moves Him, even small faith. Although we do not want to stay in small faith, it is a great place to start. We want to grow our faith, yes, but do not give up just because you think your faith is too small. Give it to God, and get ready to be amazed. Speak to that mountain, and watch it be moved! Put that seed into practice.

Fleeting Faith
My faith sat in this category of fleeting for quite some time. The definition of fleeting is brief, not lasting very long. I would have my seed of faith, throw it out, and then retreat. Let's look again at Peter walking on the water.

Shortly before dawn Jesus went out to them, walking on the lake. When the disciples saw him walking on the lake, they were terrified. "It's a ghost," they said and cried out in fear.

But Jesus immediately said to them: "Take courage! It is I. Don't be afraid."

"Lord, if it's you," Peter replied, "tell me to come to you on the water."

"Come," he said.

Then Peter got down out of the boat, walked on the water and came toward Jesus. But when he saw the wind, he was afraid and, beginning to sink, cried out, "Lord, save me!"

Immediately Jesus reached out his hand and caught him. "You of little faith," he said, "why did you doubt?"

—Matthew 14:25–31

I have felt like Peter many times when I was believing for something, bold, full of courage, taking my step toward the thing that Jesus called me to. But then in a moment, one thing or another would happen, and like a deflating balloon, my faith would spill out of me. Then I would sink because fleeting faith made me feel like I was weak. I felt like a bad Christian, not strong enough, like I should be further along already. My faith was fleeting because it was not fully convinced of the willingness and power of God on the matter.

My friend, fleeting faith does not make you less than. This is another lie from the enemy. This is a worldly view. Hear me when I say this: it is not a bad thing to be weak! It is quite the opposite, actually. It says in 2 Corinthians 12:9–11 that Christ's power is made perfect in weakness! You are not less than because you had the courage to go forward and are now sinking. This happened to Peter, the one whom Jesus later built His church on!

Sometimes the easiest part of faith is the first step. We make the declaration. We decide to believe. We are bold and full of courage. But then what about the next day? Sometimes it is the next step that is the hardest part.

How can we avoid this? We are full of faith in church but then sink in the parking lot. We could be like the disciples running around the boat thinking they are going to die, or asleep in the bottom with Jesus. We are full of faith when we are in prayer, but then we go to work and are defeated. This happens often because this is life. Life is unsteady and full of constant curve balls. "Jesus, I am believing you for the financial blessing," we say, but then the bills increase or we lose our job. "Jesus, I'm believing for the marriage," we say, but then they leave you. "Jesus, I am believing in healing," we say, but then next week we get sicker. Unlike the world, Jesus is constant and unchanging, regardless of what it looks like around you (Heb. 13:8).

I don't know about you, but I cannot afford to have my faith fleeting. I cannot afford mentally to be tossed by the waves. I cannot handle being tossed here and there; I need to be firm on my faith past the first step! We must move our faith from fleeting to fixed faith. We can do this by taking a stand.

Therefore put on the full armor of God, so that when the day of evil comes, you may be able to stand your ground, and after you have done everything, to stand. Stand firm then...
—Ephesians 6:13–14

What scriptures are you standing your faith on? What are you basing your faith on? God's words are not void. His words are a solid rock; they do not falter. His words are fruitful; they do not return to Him empty. I don't know about you, but for me, it was not enough to just say I believe God for this in my life. I had to make a stand. I had to have a courage that was not brief but instead made it past the first step, past church on Sunday, past time praying with a friend, past when it looked good and started looking bad, past the storm and the waves. Courage that was not afraid of failure. Courage that can even stand afraid. I needed a faith that could withstand it all. A faith that was built on His words, not my feelings. A faith that could withstand the storms of life.

Therefore everyone who hears these words of mine and puts them into practice is like a wise man who built his house on the rock. The rain came down, the streams rose, and the winds blew and beat against that house; yet it did not fall, because it had its foundation on the rock. But everyone who hears these words of mine and does not put them into practice is like a foolish man who built his house on sand. The rain came down, the streams rose, and the winds blew and beat against that house, and it fell with a great crash.
—Matthew 7:24–27

I needed a faith that no rain, streams, or winds could knock away. I wanted it to stand firm in every storm! Our faith is not dictated by the environment; it is set on the word of God that is forevermore (Isa. 40:8).

I did not grow up reading the Bible. I had no idea what God said about me, much less who He called me to be. I was standing on faulty grounds, ones that eventually crumbled down just like Scripture said. Those foundations could not withstand the trials of life.

I thought I would have to just deal with depression, that I would just have to live with suicidal thoughts, that it was just the cards I was dealt with. I thought I had to listen to what everyone around said about my situation, my mental health. But God did not call me to be a victim of depression and suicidal thoughts. He saved me so that I can have life—and life more abundantly. He marked me at birth for a purpose, not to be stuck in a toxic relationship. He said that I was His masterpiece, not labeled by the world. He saved me and made me for such a time as this. If that were not true, He would have let me succeed at taking my life.

I began to study what God said specifically about what I was believing for. What did God say about suicide and depression? What did God say about relationships? That is what I decided to stand on. His joy is my strength. He will give me peace that surpasses all understanding, that the world does not give to me and therefore cannot take away, that I can hide in his wings. He is my rock, my solid ground.

I made a choice to believe in something I never experienced before. Faith is believing in something not visible. It is freedom from depression. Freedom from suicide. Freedom from toxic patterns. God says in Proverbs 7:3 to "keep my words written on your heart." I had to get it on my heart. I had to know what God said about it, not what the world said, not what my own thoughts said. I needed for my faith to be attached to the word of God. My fleeting faith turned into fixed faith when I made the decision to stand on His words. When I made the decision to hear what God said about it, my faith strengthened. Romans 10:17 says, "So then, faith comes by hearing, and hearing from the Word of God."

There was no going back in the boat, and I definitely was not going to sink to the bottom of the ocean again. No plan B, only one plan: forward with a fixed faith. I had to believe that Jesus was going to fill the gap. Jesus's words were going to manifest in my life. I was going to believe it until I saw it. I had to get my fleeting faith fixed on that.

What happens often is we take a stand in faith and then start looking around and see the environment has not changed. Nothing changed around me. The storm was still loud. The rain was still beating down on me. It looked as if nothing was happening!

It is then the dangerous thoughts come in like a flood. We think, *I am following Jesus. I am trying to believe, so why is this happening to me? Wait a minute, Jesus must not have called me to this because it is way too hard. I must not have heard Him right because I feel like I am sinking. I am getting attacked from every corner, surrounded by trouble, so this must not be God. God must not want this for me.*

Lies! God wants you healed and whole! If you are not sure what the will of God is for your life, just open up the Bible and start looking. We must see past the surface. Faith is a spiritual battle.

Just because the storm has not stopped does not mean you are going in the wrong direction. It does not mean you should quit or walk away. It does not mean you are failing. Sometimes the storm might stop. But it doesn't always have to for you to have faith in it. Our environment does not dictate our faith. Our feelings do not dictate our confessions. The things going on around you do not always have to change for you to have victory over them. Do not let the storm take your faith. You have to stand firm, push past the first step. Remember His promise to you that He will uphold you with His righteous right hand (Isa. 41:10). Remember that He strengthens you when you are weak (Isa. 40:29). To get your faith from fleeting to fixed takes you standing on the word of God and being convinced of His will for your life.

Tenacious Faith

There can be times in life when your faith has to be tenacious. I mean downright crazy determined. Times when you do not care how you look or what they are saying about you. Times when the only option is to believe. Times when you absolutely need Jesus to show up. Times when you are certain that you must see this thing come to pass. Times when you must push and press to have tenacious faith.

As Jesus was on his way, the crowds almost crushed him. And a woman was there who had been subject to bleeding for twelve years, but no one could heal her. She came up behind him and touched the edge of his cloak, and immediately her bleeding stopped.

"Who touched me?" Jesus asked.

When they all denied it, Peter said, "Master, the people are crowding and pressing against you."

But Jesus said, "Someone touched me; I know that power has gone out from me."

Then the woman, seeing that she could not go unnoticed, came trembling and fell at his feet. In the presence of all the people, she told why she had touched him and how she had been instantly healed. Then he said to her, "Daughter, your faith has healed you. Go in peace."
—Luke 8:42–48

This woman was suffering for twelve years. Since she was bleeding, she was "unclean." To avoid becoming unclean themselves, men would not touch, speak to, or even look at this woman. Twelve years of isolation, of not being touched or even spoken to. Twelve years of trying to get better, doctor after doctor, remedy after remedy, spending all her money, all her time until enough was enough—until she heard that this man, Jesus, was going to be walking through her town. Until she was tired of looking for solutions and decided to believe. No matter what it took or how many people she had to get through, she was going to touch Jesus, even just the bottom of his garment. She was convinced that this was her moment. And it sure was.

In a crowd that size, there were sure to be many people suffering from all types of things. There had to be people with dying loved ones, mental-health issues, people in desperate need. But this one woman was so desperate to be healed she did whatever it took to get into the presence of Jesus. To reach out to Him. To believe for the healing. It baffles me that so many people saw Him and did not reach out to Him. Scripture even says the crowd expected Him!

Let us not be so comfortable on the sidelines that we do not even expect Jesus to do miracles in our lives. Let us not be okay with Him just passing by. Let us not be so distracted with life that we do not even hope for the dream, the business, the ministry, the healing, or the marriage anymore.

I wonder what it was that stopped them. Was it fear? Shame? Unbelief? Why did they not get healed and this one woman did? I think it was because they were not desperate enough. Maybe what they needed was serious, yes, but they were not willing to go past their comfort. They were not willing to step out. They were okay with sitting on the side in comfort. Like when Peter walked on the water, the other disciples just watched. Peter was the only one bold enough to step out. They were all just spectators, not participators. We must be crazy enough to participate! We must move past being curious about God and reach out in faith to Him. We must take the step despite the fear.

We can come to a season that we must believe that no matter how crazy we look we are going to get our healing. We are going to believe for the child. We are going to trust for the finances. We are going to have faith that God will make a way when there seems to be none. We will walk right out into the storm even when all the rest are staying in the boat. We will walk right through the crowd no matter how many people stare at us.

Faith is only crazy until it works. You might look foolish in the moment, but just you wait. What is foolish now is faith later.

To me, this scene with the healed woman lacks reason. Jesus was on His way to go perform a miracle. It does not say He was stopping to preach or lay hands on people or give a sermon. He was moving through to raise a little girl to life! But this woman was so boldly moving in faith He stopped for her. She was willing to go against the crowd and lay hands on the hem of His garment. How was she to know that His garment even healed? She was so convinced that even His clothes could heal her, convinced that He did not even have to stop but just pass by to heal her. She was crazy enough that nothing could stop her from getting to Jesus. She got her healing the others in the crowd hoped for that day as Jesus passed by. She was fully convinced, and so she was healed.

Are you fully convinced that Jesus wants you healed and whole? Convinced you can be full of joy and love? Convinced that you are valuable and worthy because He sees you that way?

Bold, tenacious faith has no plan B. It has forward-moving trust. Jesus wants you healed. Jesus wants you whole. He wants you to have everything that He has promised for you. Press into His presence. Do not just spectate but participate. Move forward with your tenacious faith. You might do it afraid, but do it. You might do it crawling, but crawl anyway. You might be limping, but limp anyway. If you are desperate enough, nothing can get in the way!

Faith Under Fire

So we talked about small faith, brief faith, and crazy faith. There comes a point in every Christian's life where, regardless of which season your faith is in, you will find it under fire. Seasons when your faith is tested, refined, and purified. I want to encourage you to go read all of Daniel 3, a great chapter of trusting Jesus in the middle of the fire. Shadrach, Meshach, and Abednego displayed great faith. When King Nebuchadnezzar tried to make them bow down to an idol, they refused and were thrown into a blazing furnace. They were convinced that God could save them, and even if He chose not to, they would only worship Him. Geez, now that is some trust.

…Shadrach, Meshach and Abednego, and these three men, firmly tied, fell into the blazing furnace.

Then King Nebuchadnezzar leaped to his feet in amazement and asked his advisers, "Weren't there three men that we tied up and threw into the fire?"

They replied, "Certainly, Your Majesty."

He said, "Look! I see four men walking around in the fire, unbound and unharmed, and the fourth looks like a son of the gods."

Nebuchadnezzar then approached the opening of the blazing furnace and shouted, "Shadrach, Meshach and Abednego, servants of the Most High God, come out! Come here!"

So Shadrach, Meshach and Abednego came out of the fire…They saw that the fire had not harmed their bodies, nor was the hair of their heads singed; their robes were not scorched, and there was no smell of fire on them.

—Daniel 3:22–27

I love this story because Jesus could have seen their faith when they chose to not bow down and stopped the fire. He could have just killed the king or destroyed the furnace. But even though He saw their faith, the three men were tied up and thrown into the fire. Jesus could have untied them and let them out, but He showed up in the fire, not just getting them out or putting it out but walking around in it. That part intrigues me. They were walking around in the fire.

Scripture talks a lot about using fire as a refining method, burning down gold so that the impurities can be removed. When things get put into fire, their forms most often change. Fire will change the way you look. It can change the way you talk, the way you walk. Fire can melt you down to your knees. Fire will burn things off you that you no longer have use for, like the ropes that were used to tie up Shadrach, Meshach, and Abednego—they were of no use anymore, so the fire got rid of them. Much like a pruning process, we must be cut back to produce more fruit. We must be refined to become pure gold.

The season of being under fire can feel as though you are, quite frankly, dying. But the fire is meant to refine your faith, not destroy it. The three men were thrown into the fire to be killed, but Jesus had another plan. God will use the very thing the enemy wanted to destroy you with to get you to the next level. He will use the fire to refine you, make you stronger, purer. He will use the chaos, the heartbreak, and the loss to build you. We must expect our faith to be put under fire.

So be truly glad. There is wonderful joy ahead, even though you must endure many trials for a little while. These trials will show that your faith is genuine. It is being tested as fire tests and purifies gold—though your faith is far more precious than mere gold. So when your faith remains strong through many trials, it will bring you much praise and glory and honor on the day when Jesus Christ is revealed to the whole world.
—1 Peter 1:6–7

How do we do this? How can we keep faith under fire? How can we remain strong in faith? To remain in faith is to remember. Remember what your stance is, not just once, not just on the first step off the boat like Peter, but daily. Strong faith requires daily focus.

Joshua 1:8 says, "Keep this Book of the Law always on your lips; meditate on it day and night, so that you may be careful to do everything written in it. Then you will be prosperous and successful." Keeping our faith when under fire is going to take intentional focus. Not just on Sundays or in front of people, not only when it is going good, but night and day! We have to remind ourselves of what we are standing on, what scriptures we are attaching our faith to.

I once read in an article from the National Science Foundation regarding research about human thoughts. The average person has about forty thousand to sixty thousand thoughts per day. Ninety-five percent of those thoughts are exactly the same repetitive thoughts as the day before. So what are your thoughts? What are you reminding yourself of? How are you reminding yourself? Scripture says in 2 Corinthians 10:5 to take your thoughts captive and arrest them. Don't let them sit there and fester. It starts with allowing one thought to sit there. It took one glance at the waves to make Peter sink.

We know that the hardest battles usually are located right in between our ears. The mind is the silent faith killer, so refuse any negative thoughts, and remind yourself of what you are believing in. Shadrach, Meshach, and Abednego reminded themselves of who their God was. He could deliver them from the fire. They did not have to even defend themselves.

Shadrach, Meshach and Abednego replied to him, "King Nebuchadnezzar, we do not need to defend ourselves before you in this matter. If we are thrown into the blazing furnace, the God we serve is able to deliver us from it, and he will deliver us from Your Majesty's hand. But even if he does not, we want you to know, Your Majesty, that we will not serve your gods or worship the image of gold you have set up."
—Daniel 3:16–18

David said to the Philistine, "You come against me with sword and spear and javelin, but I come against you in the name of the Lord Almighty, the God of the armies of Israel, whom you have defied. This day the Lord will deliver you into my hands, and I'll strike you down and cut off your head."

1 Samuel 17:45–46

King David was not standing in front of Goliath saying, "I can't do this. Maybe I should turn around. I am weak. I am the least of my brothers." David knew his stance. He knew who his God was and that with God on his side he would not fail. He was straight-up being sassy to a giant! Just like Shadrach, Meshach, and Abednego, David had this confidence about him, not because of who he was but who his God was. That is how we remain in faith under fire: we remind ourselves who God is and what He said about what we are believing for.

I know what the doctors said about me beating depression, but my God said His joy is my strength. I know that the sickness looks like it is going to take you out, but God said by His stripes you are healed. I know when they walked out on you it broke your heart, but God said He is close to the brokenhearted. They might have said you will never get the job, but promotion comes from the Lord. I know the toxic thoughts seem overwhelming, but God said He has given you the spirit of power, love, and a sound mind.

Because opposition comes, the Bible is very clear about it. *When* it comes, not *if* it comes. You need to be ready, know what you are standing on, and remind your-self of your confession, of the core scriptures you are believing for.

Take your thoughts captive, and replace them. Philippians 4:8 says, "Finally, brothers, whatever is true, whatever is honorable, whatever is just, whatever is pure, whatever is lovely, whatever is commendable, if there is any excellence, if there is anything worthy of praise, think about these things." This is what we can think about when the fire comes. True things, good things, praiseworthy things.

I know this takes work, but I can promise you that it gets easier. When I first took the stance, man, I fought hard for joy. I had to rewire some things. I did what I had to do; I did not care what it looked like. I wrote my scriptural confessions on everything: on my mirror, on my phone, on my car dashboard. Anywhere my eyes could drift, I had a reminder of what God said about it. I spoke it out loud to myself in the morning even when I did not want to. Even when friends walked away from me. Even when I had to go back to school with everyone staring at me, the crazy girl. Even when my family would walk on eggshells around me, not knowing how to talk to me. Even when I secretly wished I had been successful in taking my life, I reminded myself.

Sometimes there are no feelings attached to faith. But even when I do not feel like it, it is worth it. It is worth it to practice daily faith because it got easier eventually. I conditioned my faith to the point where I did not have to write it everywhere—it was written on me. No wave, no devil, no fire could shake me from the truth God has said to me. I was free because He set me free.

The common theme with all these faith scriptures is that Jesus is right there in the middle. Bold faith, small faith, or fleeting faith, He helps you all along the way. He never leaves you and is an ever-present help. No matter which category you find yourself in, allow Him to help you have faith with endurance. He is not offended if you need to take time to reassure yourself in the matter.

I want to encourage you no matter what stage your faith is at to take time to reassure yourself of the love and power of God. If you are believing in healing, read scriptures on healing. If you are believing for a job, read about God being your provider. If you are believing in a healthy marriage, read about how marriage is God's idea. If you are believing for kids, read about the ways God has healed the barren women. If you are believing for a sickness removed, read about how by His stripes we are healed. Get convinced, and exercise your faith, then expect to see it, not in your timing but God's perfect timing!

PRAYER:

Heavenly father, I am so grateful for your word. It is clear how important faith is. I must admit at times my faith seems in-significant and tiny. There are also times where I dismiss it altogether. Please help me develop my faith, I know that it takes consistence, but I am ready to give it my all. I want to be intentional with growing my faith. And I know that with growing comes discomfort. I pray you help me in the growth. Give me strength when I am weak. Make me strong when I want to give up. Without you, my faith simply fails but with you, my faith moves mountains. Help me believe in my heart. Help me to attach my faith to your word that is never failing. I do not want to doubt anymore. I trust you, I commit this to you. In Jesus's name, amen.

CHAPTER 10

THROUGH THE LENS

As we wrap up this journey together, I want to leave you with some really important things to remember. Some things that I am confident could change the way you live if you practice them daily. Although we may have talked about some already, I believe it is worth repeating.

It was 2018, and I was staring at my pizza, lost in thought like always. My mom and I went out for a girls' night. After one too many cheesy slices, we got onto the topic of family stories, which are some of my favorites because my big family has its fair share of funny stories. I was trying to get all of the dirt: who was the worst behaved, who was the biggest baby, who got away with the most. I was pretty much waiting for her to tell me I was the greatest child growing up. Believe it or not, that did not come out of her mouth.

She started to talk to me about my journey in these few short years. "You know, Heather, it is pretty amazing how far you have come. How different your personality is. You are strong, outgoing, independent, even social." She kept listing great things, but what she said next stuck with me most. "I can see it. Everyone around you can see it. But I am not sure that you can see it."

I wanted it to be the pizza talking, but I knew that it was the truth. Things were going great, yes. My relationship with Jesus was strengthening. My ministry was bearing fruit. My prayer life was growing. I was making improvements and doing lots of good works. But something still seemed off. I was still on the search. The search for significance, the search for purpose.

I have been on the go for over a year and a half now doing mission work. I packed up my Jeep and hit the road. I went from Florida to Los Angeles to Denver. I am now doing mission work in Sunshine Coast, Australia. I have been from job to job, couch to couch, and now country to country, all the while asking God, "What do you want for me? What is my purpose? What was the point of all this?" Nothing made sense. I was frustrated and confused. I missed my family. I missed stability. And I found myself on my knees crying out to God on the daily. On the outside, it looked like the things God had promised me were getting further and further away. I left everything and was clinging on to the dream that God put in my heart, but it seemed like nothing was happening. It seemed like I was still the broken vase on my kitchen floor. It felt like in areas that I was too shattered for Christ to fix.

So here it is, the game-changing, life-altering secret: perspective is everything. That sounds too simple to be a game changer, but I kid you not. And I am not talking about you having the right perspective, I am talking about you having a godly perspective. This walk with Christ has taught me that many things in Scripture go against the views of the world. Many things that we learn or are wired into us from a young age by society or family often are contrary to what we learn in the Bible. And what you tell yourself in your mind really, truly matters. When we align our thoughts with the word of God, our perspective can completely change. But perspective is a choice. And often to have a godly perspective is to put down our flesh in the matter.

What do I mean by that? Let me give you some examples.

My attempt at suicide. I could have the perspective that feeds the darkness in it, or I could have the perspective that uses it for His good.

I could be bitter about my troubled young adult life, or I could see ways to empathize and connect with other struggling young adults.

I could see Steven's loss of life as depression winning, or I could see it as fuel to speak up against depression. I could see it as a way to not turn a blind eye to people really hurting like we can do so easily.

Experiencing abuse and a toxic relationship with Jacob can leave me broken and damaged with trust issues, or it can push me to put God in the center of every relationship.

Trials I go through can be just dark pieces of my past or a book that has the chance to speak the love of God through each one of them. Perspective is a choice, saying, "Yeah, what is happening might quite frankly suck, but it does not determine how I react." Trials can immobilize you or propel you forward. It is perspective, looking from a different view.

I absolutely love to hike. At first, I liked loop trails the best, which go in a giant circle so you are always seeing something different. But once I started doing turnaround trails, where you make it to the point of destination and turn around, they became my favorite. I began to realize when I would turn around and head back, I would see things from a whole different perspective, see things in the trail that I did not even pick up before. It is almost like a whole new trail because my point of view was now from a different position. That is the challenge I want to leave you with: Change position. Change perspective.

This might seem simple, but many times it takes consistent effort. It takes being intentional. It takes being a "doer" of the word. Not just reading scriptures or being able to recite them—although that is amazing and is a great place to start—but putting them into practice is the next step.

But be doers of the word, and not hearers only, deceiving yourselves. For if anyone is a hearer of the word and not a doer, he is like a man who looks intently at his natural face in a mirror. For he looks at himself and goes away and at once forgets what he was like. But the one who looks into the perfect law, the law of liberty, and perseveres, being no hearer who forgets but a doer who acts, he will be blessed in his doing.

—James 1:22–25

To perceive is to be aware. I am sure you are aware that the world we live in can be dark, broken, painful, and many other things. We are constantly aware of the bad things, the hardships, the breathtaking things. The challenge is the perspective. In every storm, in every fire, in every valley, there are multiple views.

I want to view daily trials with a Christlike lens. How do we do that? Through learning the nature of Christ and disciplining our mind. I will give you some of the perspectives I try to view things from, even the crappy things. The key is *try*—I do not always get it right. But God gives us grace. The scripture above says "being no hearer who forgets but a doer who acts, he will be blessed in his doing." God blesses your efforts and extends you grace when you miss the mark. Ask God to help you on this challenge, to see Him in everyday life and see from His lens, to help align your mind with His. Hear me when I say do not get discouraged if the environment does not change; remember, the storm does not always stop. But just like turning around on the hike, the mountain didn't change—only my view of it did. God can give you grace to walk over the storm. He can give you peace in the midst. Things could still be falling around you, but He sets your feet on solid ground.

So let's start with the greatest one: perspective with love.

God Loves You

But you, Lord, are a compassionate and gracious God, slow to anger, abounding in love and faithfulness.
—Psalms 86:15

Love is tossed around these days, and at many times, it can be the cause of the biggest pains. Divorce rates are overwhelming. Kids being raised with either one or no parents is too common. Love can be often swapped out for lust. Many just toss love out as unobtainable because it has been portrayed so inaccurately by society and all those darn romantic comedies.

But the love God has for you is beyond compare. It cannot be contained in some box; it is too large to fathom. When everyone has given up on you, He has not. He loves you so much that He sent His son to bridge the gap between you and Him. His love fills the holes left by people. His love covers you from head to toe. There is no force more powerful than it. Take time to receive that, to let your mind grasp it. I know that sometimes the damage done by someone you love is so severe you numb yourself completely. But God's love moves mountains for you. His love heals, breaks chains, and frees the enslaved. It can stop the raging sea and bring you back to life. Before you even were a thought in your parents' heads, He loved you. He transcribed your life. He wants the best for you. Please take time to get fully convinced of this so you can see from the perspective you are loved by your creator so you can operate from a place of love, not a place of deficit; so you can overflow with love, not be lacking in pain.

Christ Is Alive in You—You Are Enough

But because of his great love for us, God, who is rich in mercy, made us alive with Christ even when we were dead in transgressions—it is by grace you have been saved.
—Ephesians 2:4–5

You can go anywhere and feel empty. You can get all sorts of accolades and feel like you are not enough. Follow God but still feel like you are hidden in isolation. Feel like you aren't making a difference. Feel like you aren't moving in purpose.

Christ has already placed in you what He wants to do through you. You have everything you need. We do not have to be constantly looking externally because it is already at work internally. "…for it is God who works in you to will and to act in order to fulfill his good purpose" (Phil. 2:13). We cannot find our value out in the world. Our value is in who we are in Christ. Let's look at some scriptures to help explain this.

As evening approached, the disciples came to him and said, "This is a remote place, and it's already getting late. Send the crowds away, so they can go to the villages and buy themselves some food."

Jesus replied, "They do not need to go away. You give them something to eat."

"We have here only five loaves of bread and two fish," they answered.

"Bring them here to me," he said. And he directed the people to sit down on the grass. Taking the five loaves and the two fish and looking up to heaven, he gave thanks and broke the loaves. Then he gave them to the disciples, and the disciples gave them to the people. They all ate and were satisfied, and the disciples picked up twelve basketfuls of broken pieces that were left over. The number of those who ate was about five thousand men, besides women and children.

—Matthew 14:15–21

Jesus used five loaves and the two fish that they already had in front of them to bless thousands of people. The disciples wanted to send everyone off, for people to get food elsewhere. They said no way did they have enough, but the food was right there all along. The only key was they had to bring it to Jesus. What they tossed aside as insignificant is the very thing Jesus wanted to use.

Now the wife…cried out to Elisha, "Your servant, my husband, is dead. You know that your servant honored the Lord with fear. But the man to whom he owed money has come to take my two children to make them serve him." Elisha said to her, "What can I do for you? Tell me, what do you have in the house?" And she said, "Your woman servant has nothing in the house except a jar of oil." Then he said, "Go around and get jars from all your neighbors. Get empty jars, many of them. Then go in and

shut the door behind you and your sons. Pour the oil into all these jars, and set aside each one that is full." So she went from him and shut the door behind her and her sons. They took the jars to her, and she poured. When the jars were full, she said to her son, "Bring me another jar." And he said to her, "There is not one jar left." Then the oil stopped flowing. She came and told the man of God. And he said, "Go and sell the oil and pay what you owe. You and your sons can live on the rest."
—2 Kings 4:1–7

This woman was in desperate need for a miracle. She was on the verge of losing everything, even her children. When Elisha asked her, "What do you have already?" she replied, "Nothing but a little jar of oil." When she brought her "nothing but" to Jesus, it went from *nothing but* to overflow and more than enough.

I am not sure what you are discrediting or counting out, what God has placed in you that He wants to use to not only bless you but those around you, what you disqualify because you think it will never amount to anything, what seems like an impossible thing for Jesus to use. I am not sure if you have been told that you will never make it in the industry or that you are just not smart enough. I am not sure if your dream has been chewed up or spit out. What I do know is that with Christ in you, you have more than enough. When you take your little and put it in His hands, miracles happen, people are blessed, ministry is created. With Christ in you, all things are possible.

Let the pressure fall off you. Start looking inward, not obsessing about outward.

God Fights for You
The LORD will fight for you, and you have only to be silent.
   —Exodus 14:14

Now, in all these things we are more than conquerors through him who loved us.
   —Romans 8:37

Have you ever been in a fight where you were going to lose? Lose the argument. Lose your stance. That before even going into the battle you knew it was stacked against you; there was just no way, no chance you were going to get out, much less on the winning end. You were the underdog, and this was not going to be pretty. It didn't matter how much you talked yourself up in the mirror or even if you wrote out your points. The odds were simply against you; it was like the jury was already set.

Still, you show up for the fight again and again. After all, you are tenacious. But again and again you leave the battle licking your wounds, head hanging low, feeling defeated, deciding next time you might not even show up for it.

This was my battle for some very long years. My battle to prove myself. My battle with mental health. This was me in many battles until I learned the battles are already fixed. Jesus already won this for me back on the cross.

Your fight you keep showing up to is won. Even the one you don't show up for anymore is defeated. You can walk around with the stance of victory because God is for you. When the world says no, He says yes. When your insecurity is loud, His truth will not be shaken. When it looks impossible, He says it is possible. When you give up, He picks you back up. You have the victory with Christ. When all the odds are stacked against you, He is still faithful. When the doctor's report shows up bad, He is still your healer.

I can already see the skeptics now, readers who are trying to not roll their eyes. *Yeah, Heather, you say all these things, but...*

I am not telling you these things to convince you. I am telling you these things because I have seen them all come to pass in my life. I am by no means saying that my life is all sunshine and laughter. I have days that seem to be nothing but rain and hurdles. The difference now than when I let depression and darkness rule my life is that I know Christ is right there with me holding me up, just like He is there for you. He is there nudging you forward. He is there watching your back. I know that you can have peace in the midst of chaos because your peace does not come from the world. You can have love in your heart even when someone has greatly wronged you. You can stir joy and thankfulness in your heart when situations look bleak. Trials and battles do come, sometimes many at once. But you can fight from a stance of victory just like David when he showed up to Goliath mouthing off. You can show up knowing Jesus did the heavy lifting already.

I pray as we wrap up that you are fully convinced of the goodness of God. If you are not, then I pray that this book has stirred up something in you that is going to make you dive into strengthening your relationship with Him. And I mean a burning desire that is undoubtedly a nudge from the Holy Spirit. From these pages, I pray you seek Jesus to not only heal your body but heal your soul.

If you have never asked Jesus to come into your heart and you want to start this relationship with Him, then there is no better time than right now. If that is you, I encourage you to pray this aloud:

> Jesus, I need you. I want to build a relationship with you. I often miss the mark, and I am tired of doing things my way. Thank you for loving me even in this broken state. Thank you for going to the cross for me and defeating it. I invite you in my heart to be my Lord and my Savior. I am committing myself to you. I am so excited to get to know you and your love. Holy Spirit, make me whole. Help me to trust you and grow in wisdom. In Jesus's name, amen.

Praise God! This is the best decision you can make! Now go and tell someone about it!

Just because this book is coming to an end does not mean our journey together is. In the back of this book, you can find resources to use to get connected and start on your relationship with Jesus or to join a transparent online family to help you through difficult times. If this book has helped you in any way, do not keep it to yourself—please share it!

Love always, Heather

RESOURCES

Get Connected
transparentHB.blog
(Stay tuned for my next book, *Love Letters*!)

Bible Verses
https://www.biblegateway.com/

Suicide-Prevention Line
https://suicidepreventionlifeline.org/

BOOK RECOMMENDATIONS

Study Bibles – https://www.tyndale.com: There is no better tool or book than the Bible. Study Bibles and context studies have helped me when trying to get a deeper understanding of Scripture.

Battlefield of the Mind – **Joyce Myers**: This book is a very powerful tool I reference often. Myers, using scriptures and testimony, shows us how to deal with abnormal thinking patterns and how to overcome a toxic thought life.

Switch on Your Brain – **Dr. Caroline Leaf**: I strongly encourage you to read this book; it's an absolute game changer. She uses medical research and biblical principles to draw out just how powerful our minds are. Add it to your must-reads!

GET INTO A GROUP!

In my beginning years of my walk with Christ and my battle with mental health, small groups and counseling were key. I got connected into a local church called Church by the Glades, and I do not know where I would be without the relationships I made along the way. I was so afraid to even go in the building I would sit in the parking lot without getting out of my car. The idea of small groups terrified me, but I took steps and eventually made it into the door. I have made lifelong friends, mentors, and family. Get into a group where you are—I promise it gets easier. Do not do life without a faith-filled family!

BIBLIOGRAPHY

Dennis Merritt Jones, *Your Redefining Moments: Becoming Who You Were Born to Be.* New York: Tarcher, 2015.

Lightning Source UK Ltd.
Milton Keynes UK
UKHW020653270820
368917UK00015B/523